INTERPRETING BIBLICAL TEXTS

PSALMS

GENERAL EDITORS

Gene M. Tucker, *Old Testament*

Charles B. Cousar, *New Testament*

INTERPRETING

I · B · T

BIBLICAL TEXTS

PSALMS

William P. Brown

ABINGDON PRESS

Nashville

PSALMS

Copyright © 2010 by Abingdon Press

Library of Congress Cataloging-in-Publication Data

Brown, William P., 1958-
   Psalms / William P. Brown.
      p.   cm.
   Includes bibliographical references and index.
   ISBN 978-0-687-00845-2 (binding: book- pbk./trade pbk. : alk. paper)
1. Bible. O.T. Psalms—Criticism, interpretation, etc. I. Title.
   BS1430.52.B75 2010
   223'.2066—dc22

                                                    2010005832

10 11 12 13 14 15 16 17 18 19—10 9 8 7 6 5 4 3 2 1

MANUFACTURED IN THE UNITED STATES OF AMERICA

CONTENTS

FOREWORD

Biblical texts create worlds of meaning and invite readers to
enter them. When readers enter such textual worlds, which
are often strange and complex, they are confronted with
theological claims. With this in mind, the purpose of this series is
to help serious readers in their experiences of reading and interpreting, to provide guides for their journeys into textual worlds.
The controlling perspective is expressed in the operative word of
the title—*interpreting*. The primary focus of the series is not so
much on the world behind the texts or out of which the texts have
arisen (though these worlds are not irrelevant) as on the world
created by the texts in their engagement with readers.

Each volume addresses two questions. First, what are the critical issues of interpretation that have emerged in the recent history of scholarship to which serious readers of the texts need to be
sensitive? Some scholars' concerns are interesting and significant
but, frankly, peripheral to the interpretative task. Others are more
central. How they are addressed influences decisions readers
make in the process of interpretation. Thus, the authors call
attention to these basic issues and indicate their significance for
interpretation.

Second, in struggling with particular passages or sections of
material, how can readers be kept aware of the larger world created by the text as a whole? How can they both see the forest and
examine the individual trees? How can students encountering
the story of David and Bathsheba in 2 Samuel 11 read it in light
of its context in the larger story, the Deuteronomistic History
that includes the books of Deuteronomy through 2 Kings? How
can readers of Galatians fit what they learn into the theological

coherence and polarities of the larger perspective drawn from all the letters of Paul? Each volume provides an overview of the literature as a whole.

The aim of the series is clearly pedagogical. The authors offer their own understandings of the issues and texts but are more concerned about guiding the reader than engaging in debates with other scholars. The series is meant to serve as a resource, alongside other resources such as commentaries and specialized studies, to aid students in the exciting and often risky venture of interpreting biblical texts.

Gene M. Tucker
General Editor, *Old Testament*

Charles B. Cousar
General Editor, *New Testament*

PREFACE

This book is no *Einleitung* or formal introduction to the Psalms, at least in any traditional sense. It is more invitational than introductory, more show-and-tell than textbook material. There are, for example, no separate chapters about the history of interpretation or, more specifically, about the history of scholarship, although I do acknowledge on occasion how I stand on the shoulders of those who have advanced the study of Psalms throughout the past century. Instead, this book presents a series of interrelated approaches in which the Psalms can be fruitfully interpreted by a new generation of students. By no means is it comprehensive. Rather, this modest "introduction" is more heuristic and suggestive than definitive and detailed. I have written it with students in mind, myself included. The structure of the book reflects something of my own pedagogical approach to the Psalms. One thing I have learned over the years from teaching the Bible, and the Psalms in particular, is that the best resources in the classroom, including textbooks, are the ones that create space for teaching and discussion; they do not attempt to provide all the answers or supply all the information. There is much to be said about leaving something for the reader's critical imagination. My own conclusions articulated in this book are meant to be generative, not definitive. They may also be wrong.

As evident in the table of contents, the book proceeds from poetry to theology, from the most narrow to the most integrative, from the lively microworld of interacting poetic segments to the Psalter's complex macrostructure and theological framework. Each chapter builds on the previous. Each combines discussion of method with concrete demonstration. I have found poetry to be a good place to begin (chapters 1 and 2). Modern poetry, despite significant differences from ancient poetry, can serve as a useful entrée into the beauty and power of biblical poetry. From the poetic we move to the generic, the staple of Psalms study over the years. By making this move, the reader steps back from the smallest unit of psalmic expression, the poetic line, to view the psalm in its entirety as defined by its generic shape (chapter 3). Of course, no discussion of genre would be complete without discussing how various psalms could have functioned, and can function, performatively within their implied settings or *Sitze* and even beyond them (chapter 4). One thing that distinguishes my treatment from others is the conviction that reading the Psalms as poetry is as performative as using them liturgically. There is no need, as I see it, to drive the wedge ever deeper that separates *reading* the Psalms from *using* them. In the ancient world, reading was reciting, and "meditating" was manifest in discursive activity (see Ps 1:2). Reading the Psalms, I argue, is no passive enterprise.

The remaining chapters continue to expand the interpretive purview. Chapter 5 looks at the Psalms in terms of their various collections and groupings—some defined by their superscriptions, reflecting haphazard arrangements, others by thematic and intertextual links, subtle though they may be. How certain psalms within a given cluster interact, whereby one psalm interprets another or various psalms together present a distinctive profile of the speaker or of God, is the focus of this chapter. Spinning the hermeneutical web ever wider, chapter 6 addresses the ways the Psalms can be read as a whole, that is, as a "book," a topic of much recent discussion. On the one hand, nothing prevents one from reading the Psalms as a book. On the other hand, reading the Psalms as a whole is no easy matter, and there is no one way of doing so. Whether the final editors intended the Psalter to be a book—that is, to be read from beginning to end for, say, moral instruction or as devotional inspiration—remains an open question, but I believe such was their intent in part. In any case, chapter 6 illustrates one possible way of reading the Psalter, from *tôrâ* (Ps 1) to praise (Ps 150).

The final chapter also takes up the Psalter as a whole, but for the purpose of discerning the complex character of God and humankind profiled in the book. Some argue that the search for a coherent profile of God in the Psalms is impossible, even mis-guided. I fully acknowledge the Psalter's diversity of perspectives on God by reviewing the various genres featured in the Psalter and identifying how each one presents a distinctive profile of the God who is addressed in complaint, praised in acclamation, and proclaimed didactically. Nevertheless, these differing portraits are interrelated. More challenging, however, is discerning the theo-logical relevance of the harsh imprecation psalms. This, too, is addressed.

Finally, a postscript is included that offers a constructive, over-arching metaphor by which to see (and hear) the Psalter as a whole, an image that I have found helpful in appropriating and teaching the Psalms anew. It is one that invites me time and again to reenter the challenging, edifying, disturbing world of the Psalms. Interpreting psalms is an ongoing process of entry and reentry, of listening and relistening, of taking part in a perfor-mance that never turns out to be the same.

A final note to the reader: interpreting the Psalms has its host of challenges, but a particularly annoying one is more logistical than theological. It has to do with the numbering of psalms and their verses. There are two systems of numbering the Psalms, one drawn from the Hebrew (Masoretic) text (MT) and the other from the Greek Septuagint (LXX). The latter counts Psalms 9–10 and 114–115 as single psalms, and divides Psalms 116 and 147 into two psalms apiece. The result is a discrepancy between the Greek and Hebrew textual traditions between Psalms 9 and 147. The Latin Vulgate and the old Roman Catholic Bibles follow the Septuagint numbering, whereas all modern translations follow the Hebrew numbering. The Septuagint, moreover, contains a final psalm, Psalm 151, that is unattested in the Masoretic tradition. The study will follow the Hebrew numbering of the Psalms.

As for verse numbering, the Hebrew text and most English edi-tions differ significantly for many of the psalms because the Hebrew frequently counts the superscription as the first verse. Not so in the English. Thus, every interpreter is faced with a choice about how to identify the verses in translation and in dis-cussion. In view of my intended audience, I have chosen to use English versification, even though the translations featured in this book reflect my own work with the Hebrew.

ABBREVIATIONS

ANET   *Ancient Near Eastern Texts Relating to the Old Testament.* Edited by J. B. Pritchard. Princeton, 1969

AOTC   Abingdon Old Testament Commentaries

BETL   Bibliotheca ephemeridum theologicarum lovaniensium

BHS   *Biblia Hebraica Stuttgartensia.* Edited by K. Elliger and W. Rudolph. Stuttgart, 1983

BM   Benjamin R. Foster. *Before the Muses: An Anthology of Akkadian Literature.* 2 vols. 2d ed. Bethesda, 1996

CBQ   *Catholic Biblical Quarterly*

ECC   Eerdmans Critical Commentary

FOTL   Forms of the Old Testament Literature

HALOT   Koehler, L., W. Baumgartner, and J. J. Stamm. *The Hebrew and Aramaic Lexicon of the Old Testament.* Study Edition. 2 vols. Leiden, 2001

HAT   Handbuch zum Alten Testament

JBL   *Journal of Biblical Literature*

JBR   *Journal of Bible and Religion*

JSOT   *Journal for the Study of the Old Testament*

JSOTSup	Journal for the Study of the Old Testament: Supplement Series
LH	Laws of Hammurabi
LHB/OTS	Library of Hebrew Bible/Old Testament Studies
LXX	Septuagint
MT	Masoretic Text
NIV	New International Version
NRSV	New Revised Standard Version
SBLDS	Society of Biblical Literature Dissertation Series
SBLWAW	Society of Biblical Literature Writings from the Ancient World
STDJ	Studies on the Texts of the Desert of Judah
VTSup	Supplements to Vetus Testamentum
ZAW	*Zeitschrift für die alttestamentliche Wissenschaft*

CHAPTER 1

PSALMS AS POETRY: PROSODY

*Poetry cannot be read, I would argue; it can only be
reread. For me, it is a continuation of the holy scriptures.*
                                                    —Jay Parini[1]

A painter once engaged the nineteenth-century French poet Stéphane Mallarmé with the following complaint: "I have tried to write poetry, but I cannot do it, even though I have ever so many ideas." Mallarmé responded, *"Chéri,* poems are not written with ideas, but with words."[2] Mallarmé was right: words are the essence of poetry, words used in very special ways. Arguments and treatises, however rhetorically embellished, can be boiled down to their logical, or fallacious, ideas. Narratives can be summarized with synopses. Poetry, however, resists such reductions. The study of poetry is fundamental to the study of Psalms, and to introduce the poetic nature of ancient Hebrew psalmody, we begin with modern poetry.

Modern Poetry

Defining poetry, whether ancient or modern, is an elusive endeavor. "Poetry is the kind of thing poets write," said Robert Frost.[3] Such an operational "definition" simply pushes the question back a step: so what defines a poet? Arriving at a conclusive, fits-all-sizes definition is impossible. Nevertheless, one can identify certain features that help distinguish a poem from a narrative or an argument: (1) artistic or aesthetic quality; (2) density or compactness of expression; (3) performative power.

Aesthetic Quality

"Poem" comes from the Greek verb *poieō*, "make" or "do." A poem is a literary, indeed artistic, creation. It is not mechanically or casually produced. Poetry is verbal art. A poem is crafted to be impressive to the ear; its diction is frequently conveyed through the use of assonance and alliteration as well as through its metrical structure or rhythm. Such poetic devices serve to "thicken the verbal texture" of a poem.[4]

In addition, there is the visual side to the verbal aesthetic. The format of a poem, for example, distinguishes itself from prose narrative: much shorter lines and uneven right margins for English poems. Poetry is arranged in lines instead of paragraphs. As the most basic unit of poetry, the line is typically absent in straight prose. As we shall see in biblical poetry, a verse largely consists of parallel or corresponding lines. And there is another critical aspect to a poem's graphic texture. More often than not, poems revel in imagery and metaphor, in figurative language and allusion. A poem evokes images and feelings that stir the imagination. The attuned reader not only *hears* the poem in all its eloquence but also *sees* in and through the poem all that it conjures in the reader's mind. A poem is not only riveting to the ear; it is also arresting to the eye. What makes a poem a poem is its synergy between sense and sound.

Density of Expression

A poem typically has less space to wield its communicative craft than its prose counterpart. With the exception of epic poetry, a poem is generally short and compact. Its terseness is its literary hallmark. The German term for poetry is *Dichtung,* which coincidentally sounds as it if were derived from the German *dicht,* meaning "dense."[5] According to J. P. Fokkelman, "poetry is the most compact and concentrated form of speech possible,"[6] with the exception, I would add, of electronic text messaging. The difference between a poem and an instruction manual is readily evident: a poem's terse style conveys an abundance of meaning. Laurence Perrine defines poetry as "a kind of language that says *more* and says it more intensely than does ordinary language."[7] More "condensed and concentrated" than prose, poetry exhibits a "higher voltage" and applies "greater pressure per word."[8] A poem, thus, marks the convergence of verbal compactness and semantic intensity. Semantically, poetry does a lot of heavy lifting, and with its semantic abundance comes ambiguity. More than any other form of discourse, poetry invites multiple readings. Much in contrast to a text message, a poem conveys a palpable richness that resists a narrowing of meaning. Poetic language is generously and generatively suggestive.[9]

Performative Power

The words, images, and rhythms of a poem invite the reader to feel, sense, and imagine. In poetry, the reader is brought into intimate relationship with the poem's speaking voice. The reader performs the poem in the very act of reading, and the kind of performative reading that a poem requires is first and foremost a close and careful reading, an attentive recitation. A poem lends itself first to recitation and only thereafter to interpretation. A poem must be sounded, otherwise its palpably oral quality is lost; its rhythm and rhyme, its assonance and euphony, are grossly disregarded. Such qualities have compelled many to compare poetry to music.[10] Both typically share a sense of rhythm. Many of Emily Dickinson's poems, for example, can be sung to the tune of "Amazing Grace," although they were not intended for such use. It is no coincidence that many of the biblical psalms are given instructions for what appears to be musical accompaniment.[11] As S. E. Gillingham notes, "To understand Hebrew poetry at all, we have to participate imaginatively in its performative power.... The psalms have an evocative power; they communicate beyond the boundaries of ancient Israel, and continuously testify to a capacity to perform their one 'score.' "[12] Activated by the reader's imagination, a poem's performative power is its power to evoke. As a result, a poem transcends the poet's own context, allowing it to join the ranks of all poetic works, ancient and modern, Eastern and Western.

Reading a poem is quite different from reading a narrative or an essay. Poetry "is not to be galloped over like the daily news: a poem differs from most prose in that it is to be read slowly, carefully, and attentively."[13] A poem places a high demand on the reader's active participation. To read a poem as poetry is to linger over the words, to reflect on their sequence, to read aloud for their assonance and alliteration as they roll off, or get stuck on, the tongue. There is an element of simultaneity when it comes to reading poetry. As we read, the poem unfolds before our eyes and ears, and as the poem unfolds, so does our reading. The art of reading poetry is to find oneself "moving inside the growing poem."[14] We do not read to impose our meaning on the poem or to extract something out of it. Rather, as Mary Kinzie points out, "We are actively remaking the work's own meaning, tracing the path of the poem from among the tangle of possible routes it might have taken but did not. In effect, we accompany the poet through the ambiguous emergence of the eventual artistic pattern."[15] In short, reading poetry is much like writing poetry: it proceeds thoughtfully and creatively, word by word, image by image, beat by beat.

These three features of poetry, while briefly discussed above as discrete topics, are inseparably wedded in any good piece of poetry. Together, they ensure a poem's freshness and openness to interpretation that other discursive genres do not necessarily feature, at least not to the degree that poetry does. Kinzie talks of poetry as "a sequence of new turnings" that is "neither the clone of a convention nor a mere wildcat product of will."[16] Poetry does its work by bringing out something new from what is conventional. "Most poetry is the product of experiments on the past, acts of recombining already invented substances in such a way that they are transformed."[17] The poet is a semantic alchemist who combines standard verbal ingredients in new ways and records the surprising results. He or she excels in the art of combination, of juxtaposition. A poem's freshness emerges from the forging of new connections among familiar words and images, from taking surprising turns along well-worn routes. "The best poems satisfy

4

by surprise, either because they reject something more familiar, or because they teeter on the edge of confusion in knowing something else."[18]

Something mysterious transpires when reading a poem, as X. J. Kennedy and Dana Gioia admit: "For, when we finish reading a good poem, we cannot explain precisely to ourselves what we have experienced—without repeating, word for word, the language of the poem itself."[19] The irreducible nature of poetry provides a necessary check on all methods of interpretation. In the end, no method or combination of methods will ever fully approximate the full sense and sound of poetic verse. They all fall short of capturing something of the ineffable that poetry conveys. Perhaps that is why the psalmists found it most appropriate to speak to God and of God through the medium of poetry.

Hebrew Poetry

Now that we have examined some of the defining marks of modern poetry, what about ancient biblical poetry? Like modern poetry, the poetry of the Psalms can be at once conventional and innovative. On the one hand, the language of prayer and praise is stereotypical and repetitive, drawing from stock vocabulary and set styles. Many psalms, moreover, exhibit identifiable patterns, or "forms," by which their literary movement is largely determined. On the other hand, psalmic poetry can sparkle with unexpected imagery and striking semantic connections established through the creative juxtaposition of words and lines. Behind every psalm, behind every cry of praise and petition, is a poet, a weaver of words whose tapestry may at first glance seem conventional and generic, yet upon closer scrutiny can elicit something new for the reader to experience, indeed a "new song" to sing.

Reading for Rhythm: Meter?

Like poetry in general, the Psalms reflect a compact style of discourse, employ figurative language, and evoke powerful images and emotions. Grammatically, the terse language of biblical poetry tends to omit certain linguistic elements frequently found in Hebrew prose, such as the definite article, relative pronouns, and the direct object marker, to name a few. In addition to what biblical poetry lacks, there are certain features that also distinguish, in relative degree, biblical poetry from prose: for example, line structure, peculiar word order, greater assonance and alliteration (even rhyme on occasion), repetition, chiasmus, unusual vocabulary, and word pairs. Note that "meter" is not included in the list. To be sure, both modern poetry and ancient Hebrew poetry reflect what is called prosody, but they can do so in different ways. Broadly put, prosody refers to a poem's movement in verbal time.[20] Derived from the Greek word for "accent," the term is more specifically used to describe a poem's "auditory logic," or set rhythmic style, as determined by an identifiable system of stresses, such as iambic pentameter.

Hebrew poetry, however, rarely adheres to a uniform metrical *system*. Scholars have tried to adopt the system of iambic meter (whereby the stress or accent of a word falls on the second syllable) for Hebrew poetry, but with mixed results. In some cases, accentual rhythms have been successfully identified, such as the so-called *qînāh* or "lamentation," in which a divisible line of poetry features an accentual beat of 3:2 (see, e.g., Amos 5:2; Ps 5:1-2; much of Lamentations). Some read Psalm 117, the shortest psalm in the Psalter, as reflecting a consistent rhythm of 3:3.[21] But such a count depends on how one assigns the accents, particularly in construct chains. Others have counted syllables to determine prosodic regularity, but again with mixed success. While Psalm 113 reflects syllabic consistency,[22] most other psalms do not, unless one resorts to emending the text to fit a particular count. The issue of meter in Hebrew poetry, thus, remains open. As Wilfred Watson points out, "Confusion arises because scholars fail to distinguish between metre as actually present in verse, and *regular* metre. There is metre, yes, but not regular metre, since metrical patterns are never maintained for more than a few verses at a stretch, if even that."[23] Although meter is clearly evident in biblical Hebrew poetry, it varies far too much to permit the identification of a metrical system.

Reading between the Lines: Parallelism

A more fruitful line of inquiry (particularly for readers not familiar with Hebrew) is to examine the syntactic and semantic segmentation of lines in biblical poetry. The history of early textual transmission gives telling, albeit mixed, testimony. Among the Dead Sea Scrolls, a psalter from Cave IV dated to mid-second century B.C.E (4QPs[a]) features psalms consistently set in prose format or continuous script, that is, without separated lines. However, fragments of another scroll (4QPs[b], dated in the second half of the first century B.C.E) feature poetic lines written in stichometric or line-structured arrangement.[24] Jump ahead about a thousand years and we find the Leningrad Codex (1009 C.E), upon which the standard critical edition of the Hebrew Bible (*BHS*) is currently based, featuring a few psalms set in stichometric form (Pss 117; 118:1-4; 119; 135:19-20; 136). In an earlier codex, the Aleppo Codex (925 C.E), Psalm 1 is written in prose format, as is also Chronicles, which immediately precedes it, but Psalm 2 is set in stichometric structure. It appears, then, that both formatting traditions coexisted in the transmission of biblical psalms, at least since the first century B.C.E. But regardless of the lack of consistency reflected in ancient manuscripts, stichometric structure in Hebrew verse is ultimately based on internal grounds, specifically on internal segmentation.

This defining characteristic of Hebrew poetry has captured the attention of modern interpreters for more than two centuries. Robert Lowth, professor of poetry at Oxford University, published his lectures *De sacra poesi Hebraeorum* ("On the Sacred Poetry of the Hebrews") in 1753, setting the course for much subsequent research in biblical poetry. In his lectures, Lowth explored the aesthetic dimensions of Hebrew poetry, which in his words exhibit an "exquisite degree of beauty and grace."[25] Lowth identified what he considered to be the central feature of biblical poetry, *parallelismus membrorum* ("parallelism of parts"). Poetic parallelism reflects "a certain conformation of the sentences."[26] It conveys "the same thing in different words, or different things in a similar form of words."[27] In 1778, Lowth gave a more precise definition of this linguistic phenomenon in his "preliminary dissertation" on Isaiah: "The correspondence of one verse, or line with another, I call parallelism."[28] In other words, such correspondence is evident in the way the segments within any given verse of poetry "answer" or talk to one another.[29] Lowth placed these poetic correspondences into three broad categories: synonymous, antithetic, and synthetic parallelism.[30]

A few examples will suffice. A Hebrew verse typically consists of two segments, sometimes referred to as "bicola," although triplets ("tricola") and more elaborate patterns are also attested. In a

7

typical poetic couplet, the second segment (colon or stich) can repeat, intensify, modify, or complete the thought of the first. Furthermore, the relationship between the two cola may not always be obvious or even parallel in any strict sense. Yet such regular pairing of segments conveys a sense of lyrical symmetry. Take, for example, the sentence in Ps 114:1-2, translated in strict Hebrew word order (with the subject typically following the verb):

> When went forth Israel from Egypt,
>> the house of Jacob from a people of unintelligible
>>> speech,
> became Judah God's sanctuary,
>> Israel his dominion.

The extended circumstantial clause (v. 1) consists of two parallel "cola," which could be labeled A and A', in which "Israel" and "house of Jacob" serve as corresponding partners, as well as "Egypt" and "a people of unintelligible speech." A succinct way of representing such correspondences is as follows:

$$A \; [a{:}b{:}c] \; / \; A' \; [b'{:}c']$$

The first colon (A) contains three grammatical elements: a circumstantial verbal phrase ("when went forth" = a), the subject ("Israel" = b), and a prepositional phrase ("from Egypt" = c). The second colon (A') features a corresponding subject ("house of Jacob" = b') and a corresponding prepositional phrase ("from a people of unintelligible speech" = c'). Lacking, however, is a corresponding verb, hence no a'. Rather, the verb is simply understood in the second colon, making it elliptical: "the house of Jacob [went forth] from a people of unintelligible speech." The second colon not only repeats the first colon; it develops the first. Lowth considered this a classic example of synonymous parallelism, a case in which poetic correspondence expresses "the same sense in different but equivalent terms."[31] At the very least, the corresponding partners establish certain relationships of identity: Israel *is* the "house of Jacob"; Egypt *is* a "people of unintelligible speech." Similarly, the main clause (v. 2), also cast in two segments, has its corresponding elements: "Judah" and "Israel," as well as "God's sanctuary" and "his dominion." Note that the second colon is also elliptical, reflecting identical prosodic structure as found in verse 1.

Another example of comparably balanced parallelism is found in Ps 30:11 (v. 12 in Hebrew).

> You have turned my wailing into dancing;
>> you have removed my sackcloth and clothed me with joy.

The second line, or colon, amplifies the first. The first employs the language of activity and emotion, whereas the second features articles of clothing. Nevertheless, correspondences are clear:

$$A\ [a{:}b{:}c]\ /\ A'\ [a'{:}b'{:}a''{:}c']$$

The one anomaly in this perfectly ordered sequence of corresponding segments is the appearance of the extra verb a''. The second colon (A') features *two* complementary verbs (a' and a'') to explicate the one verb (a) featured in the first colon (A), illustrating more graphically how God has transformed the speaker's situation from lament to celebration. The negative verbal object, "mourning" (b), in the first colon finds its parallel in the image of "sackcloth" (b'), and the positive image of "dancing" (c) is associated with the apparel of "joy" (c').

Both examples illustrate Lowth's classification of "synonymous" parallelism. But as can be readily seen, more is going on than simple repetition. There is a movement or interchange between the two cola. Through the positive pairing of cola and their corresponding parts, one colon amplifies, expands on, or explicates the other. Poetic momentum builds from the first to the second.

Examples of Lowth's "antithetical" type of parallelism exhibit correspondence "when two lines correspond with one another by an opposition of terms and sentiments; when the second is contrasted with the first."[32] This can readily be seen in the following two examples:

> For you a lowly people deliver,[33]
>> *but* haughty eyes you bring down. (18:27 [Heb v. 28])

> Some in chariotry, others in horses,
>> *but* we in the name of YHWH find strength.[34]
>>> (20:7 [Heb v. 8])

In each example, the telltale sign of "antithetical" parallelism is clearly evident in English translation. However, it is not so imme-

9

diately clear in the Hebrew. The connecting particle is the same in Hebrew (the simple *waw*), whether serving as a conjunctive ("and") or as an adversative ("but") in the second colon. Thus, context is critical. The correspondence in both examples is contrastive rather than synonymous: "humble people" and "haughty eyes" constitute an opposite pair, as do the verbal elements "deliver" and "bring down." Using for convenience the symbol of negation in the field of logic (~), we can illustrate the relationship of correspondence as A [a:b:c] ~ A' [b':c'], with (a) designating the independent personal pronoun "you" in the first colon, which is absent in the second. (The "you" in the second colon indicates a verbal inflection in Hebrew, not a separate, independent pronoun.)

Consisting of two clauses, the second example is syntactically more complex: A [a:b:a':b'] ~ A [a'':b'':c]. The first colon lacks a verb. Here is a case of the *first* colon being elliptical. The second colon supplies the verb (c), which can be read back into the first: "Some [find strength] in chariotry; others [find strength] in horses." The second colon fills the gap of the first. As a whole, the first colon sets up the foil for the second, which commends the true source of strength. In the first example, however, the foil is featured in the second colon instead of the first. In both examples, the relationship between the two cola is "antithetical," but, as in the case of so-called synonymous parallelism, more is at work than a static correspondence between opposites. Indeed, the two examples are contrastive in contrasting ways. Psalm 20:7 charts a movement from false trust to true allegiance, the latter exposing the former as illusory. The second colon deconstructs the first. In 18:27, the "antithetical" relationship between the two cola is different: both lines are held to be equally true; the second is the converse and consequence of the first. Delivering the lowly entails the humiliation of the haughty.

As for "synthetic" parallelism, Lowth recognized examples of Hebrew verse that do not fit into either of the two above-mentioned categories. Parallelism, whether synonymous or antithetical, does not apply in the following cases:

Blessed be YHWH,
who did not give us over to their teeth as prey. (124:6)

From the sun's rising to its setting,
may YHWH's name be praised. (113:3)

10

In the first example, the two cola are linked by a common subject, but that is as far as the syntactical similarity goes. The first colon invokes a blessing, for which the second, as a subordinate clause, provides the warrant. In the second example, the first colon prefaces the second, which provides its subject matter. This particular case of nonparallel lines exhibits *enjambment* (literally "straddling"), whereby a sentence or thought does not end where the first colon ends but continues naturally into the next.[35] Enjambment creates a certain " 'tugging' effect" on the reader.[36] Indeed, many of the verses Lowth considered "synthetic" consist of enjambed lines.

Lowth's method of classification has its limitations. Like form-criticism, the categories Lowth defined can foster a taxonomic mentality that misses rather than elucidates the "exquisite degree of beauty and grace" he discerned in Hebrew poetry. Nevertheless, his central observation endures: Hebrew poetry often consists of corresponding or contiguous segments, that is, parallel parts. We have found that the correspondences are more nuanced than Lowth evidently thought. The term "synonymous," for example, is misleading if it simply means repetition. The same can also be said of "antithetical" and "synthetic"—classifications too general or rigid to be very helpful. As James Kugel readily points out, even in the most "synonymous" poetic lines there is a semantic climax found in the "seconding" role of colon B, which can serve to emphasize or advance the thought: "A is so, and *what's more*, B is so."[37]

Parallelism, specifically the *"predominance* of parallelism, combined with terseness," is a defining mark of Hebrew poetry.[38] And it need not be limited to semantic pairs. Parallelism is evident on any number of linguistic levels, from phonology and morphology to syntax and semantics.[39] With the exception of enjambed lines, juxtaposed poetic segments are contiguous; rarely is one syntactically subordinated to the other. This quality of contiguity is commonly referred to as "paratactic" style: segments coordinated without connecting particles. But whether paratactic or not, Hebrew poetry thrives on parallelism. If, as Paul Valéry claims, "Poetry is to prose as dancing is to walking,"[40] then Hebrew poetry is typically a two-step.

Merely identifying various levels of correspondence between cola is one thing; charting the progression from one colon to the next is something else. The result is a change of meaning, however subtle. Robert Alter quotes Viktor Shklovsky regarding the purpose of parallelism: "to *transfer* the usual perception of an object into the sphere of a new perception—that is, to make a unique semantic modification."[41] A product of poetic artistry, parallelism generates in the reading process a progression of thought that can serve any number of purposes from clarification to intensification, even deconstruction. Parallelism thus highlights a complexity of correspondences, from the patently obvious to the sublimely subtle. All in all, parallelism reveals "a dynamic microworld in which many different components function in relation to each other."[42] A single colon generates only provisional meaning. In isolation, poetic cola supply only "half-meanings," and as such they prompt the reader to continue reading, thoughtfully and imaginatively, to the poem's end.[43] Poetic parallelism, in effect, carries the reader forward two (or three) steps at a time.

Psalm 147: The Exquisite Degree of Praise

By way of illustration, I have chosen Psalm 147 to show how one might analyze a psalm poetically and, thereby, reveal its "dynamic microworld" of interacting segments and surprising connections. As the first verse attests, this psalm is all about rendering "exquisite praise" to God. To examine it poetically is to experience something of the psalm's "exquisite" character. The following discussion will unfold in a twofold manner. Taking my cue from Susan Gillingham, the first step involves "looking at the poem," much like analyzing a musical score on the printed page.[44] Conducting a prosodic analysis, line by line, is key. The second step is "looking through" the poem, which involves stepping back to discern the psalm's poetic coherence—its broader contours and dynamics—and the larger world it constructs.

Text and Texture

STROPHE I (VV. 1-6)

Hallelujah!
How good it is to sing to our God!
    How delightful[45] (it is to sing) exquisite praise!
YHWH builds up Jerusalem;

12

> the outcasts of Israel he gathers up,
> who heals the brokenhearted,
>   and binds up their wounds,
> who counts the number of the stars;
>   to all of them he gives names.
> Great is our Lord and abundant in power;
>   of his understanding there is no number.
> YHWH restores the poor,
>   but casts down the wicked to the earth.[46]

The psalm begins with a one-word shout of praise: the imperative followed by its abbreviated object (translated "Praise YH").[47] But not just so simple a call to praise will do for this psalm. The command is immediately followed by a fervent commendation that ascribes supreme value to such praise. Verse 1 (without the opening imperative) can be mapped prosodically as follows: A [a:b:c] / A′ [a′:d]. While each colon is composed of four Hebrew words, achieving fine poetic symmetry, the second (A′) is cast elliptically. The first segment of each colon (a and a′) represents an acclamation ("How good/How delightful"). The second colon makes good sense if the verbal construction of the first colon (b) is understood to apply to the second: "How delightful [it is to sing] exquisite praise!" Segments (c) and (d) designate the final segments, both construed grammatically as objects (indirect and direct) of the verb "sing." The opening of each colon, introduced by the particle of exclamation, *kî* ("how"), explodes phonetically. There is, moreover, a semantic intensification from the first to second colon, from "good" (*tôb*) to "delightful" (*nāʿîm*). With such sequenced juxtaposition, the second colon shifts the poetic center of attention to the word "exquisite" (*nāʾwâ*), an aesthetically loaded term. The word marks this psalm as both aesthetically compelling and profoundly proper in the way it articulates praise. This psalm is no ordinary expression of wonder (if there is such a thing); it is special praise, proper and delightful.

Following the command and commendation of verse 1, a series of poetic lines detail the deity's role and activity, providing both the content and warrant for praise. Each line typically opens with a participle. Verse 2, for example, begins with a strong opening, namely, with the verb "build" (*bônēh*) in the following literal order in Hebrew: "builds Jerusalem YHWH." Even though the object is placed between the verb and its subject, which concludes

13

the first segment, the subject's identity is never in question. The parallelism is as follows: A [a:b:c] / A' [b':a'].

Verse 2 thus follows a chiastic arrangement in which the second colon renders in reverse the syntactical order of the first. All that is missing in the second colon is explicit reference to the deity, who is understood as the subject. The verbs bracket the two cola, forming a tight correspondence between "build" and "gather." The first verb refers to urban restoration, the second to social development. Or, to view it another way, the two cola juxtapose what is spatially central and what is peripheral: Jerusalem, the religious and political center of a nation, paired with the exiles subsisting beyond their homeland. The correspondence between the center and the periphery runs deep: the ruins of Jerusalem are matched by Israel's "outcasts," literally those who have been pushed away. Jerusalem's (re)construction and Israel's (re)gathering are poetically bound together.

Verse 3 follows in sequentially corresponding order: A [a:b] / A'[a':b']. The subject, God, is no longer stated outright, as in the two previous verses, but the participles are a dead giveaway. The first participle is definite, pointing back to the previous reference to God's proper name, YHWH, in verse 2, "*the* one who heals." The object of the first verb is literally the "broken of heart." The other verb is a fitting corollary that lends greater specificity to divine healing: God "binds up their wounds." As verse 3 follows on the heels of verse 2, a more subtle parallelism emerges: God rebuilds Jerusalem's ruins and heals the brokenhearted; God gathers outcasts and binds up open wounds. The first cola of the two verses focus on restoring what is broken, while the second cola convey a constrictive movement, of gathering and binding.

From verse 3 to verse 4 the reader is transported from damaged bodies to celestial bodies. Arranged chiastically (A[a:b:c] / A'[c':b':a']), verse 4 opens with a participle and concludes with a finite verb, just as in verse 2. The parallel cola are bound together by alliteration in (c) and (c'): *lakôkābîm* ("stars") and *lĕkullām* ("all of them"). The alliteration also confirms the antecedent of the prepositional phrase. Semantic intensification is key. Not only is the total number of stars determined, but God names them individually.

Distinct from the previous verses, verse 5 consists of two verb-less sentences. This shift in syntax reflects a different kind of

14

divine ascription. Nowhere is God's activity specifically addressed, as in the earlier verses. Rather, the verse is a general acclamation of God's greatness. It opens with explosive alliteration: *gādôl 'ădônênû* ("great is our Lord"), with emphasis on the *dalet* or "d" consonant, and the first colon ends with the tongue-stopper *kōah* ("power"). While the first colon is cast positively, its partner is articulated negatively: A [a:b:a'] / A'[b':a'']. The a-based segments refer to various dimensions of God's character. The b-based segments pair together God and God's understanding. As God's power is so abundant, God's understanding is immeasurable or without limit ("no number"). Although with similar syntax, the second colon works in reverse word order of that found in verse 4*a*. Verses 4*a* and 5*b* are bound together by the sharing of the word *mispār* ("number"), which sets the two verses off as a thematic unit, a poetic *inclusio* (vv. 4*a*, 5*b*). The juxtaposition exquisitely evokes the infinite character of the Creator's wisdom.

The strophe concludes with a resumption of participial clauses. Thematically, verse 6 hearkens back to verse 3, with its focus on sufferers, here designated as the "poor" or oppressed (*'ănāwîm*). For the first time in this psalm, the parallelism is contrastive ("antithetical"): A [a:b:c] ~ A' [a':b':d]. The contrastive relationship imbues the first verb ("help") with the sense of upward movement. The poor are raised up to be restored (cf. 146:9), but the wicked are cast down to the ground in judgment. Instead of a corresponding reference to God (c), the second colon features an additional segment (d) ("to the earth"), giving vivid force to the verb ("cast down") and prompting the reader to imagine: if the wicked are brought low to the ground, how high are the poor lifted up? To heaven? The common pairing of "heaven" and "earth" in biblical Hebrew would suggest so. In any case, the syntactical, contrastive balance of verse 6 suggests a moral, retributive balance.

STROPHE II (VV. 7-11)

Sing to YHWH with thanksgiving!
   Make melody to our God with lyre!
Who covers the heavens with clouds,
   who provides rain for the earth,
     who causes the mountains to sprout grass,
who gives to cattle their food,
   to the raven's brood as they call out.

15

No delight does he take in the strength of the horse;
  no pleasure[48] does he take in the legs of a runner.[49]
Instead, YHWH takes pleasure in those who fear him,
  in those who hope in his benevolence.[50]

The second strophe opens with a call to praise whose first word (*ʿĕnû*) phonetically resembles the word "poor" (*ʿănāwîm*) in the previous verse; both words, in fact, share the same verbal root, *ʿnh*. A wordplay is born. Verse 7 exhibits as straight a parallelism as any Hebrew verse can: A [a:b:c] / A′ [a′:b′:c′]. Both cola, moreover, share an identical syntactical sequence: imperative, object, and predicate, with one-to-one grammatical correspondence. But the correlation between the predicates "thanksgiving" and "lyre" indicates a significant pairing of differences. These complementary predicates illustrate "exquisite praise" in two distinct ways, namely, in content and style: "thanksgiving," or declarative praise, for content and accompaniment by the lyre for music. Set apart, these semantic partners do not necessarily share any overlap in meaning, let alone correspondence. But in the hands of the poet, they are tightly coordinated: music and lyric, lyre and thanksgiving, together yielding proper praise to God.

Verse 8, like verse 2, articulates the substance of, as well as the basis for, praise. The verse is structured as a tricolon, the only one in this psalm: A [a:b:c] / A′ [a′:c′:b′] / A″[a″:b″:c″]. Each colon opens with a definite participle: "who covers . . . , who provides . . . , who causes to sprout," each highlighting an aspect of God's work in creation to ensure the earth's fertility. A logical progression is evident in the sequential ordering of the three cola: clouds, rain, and grass. Together, they mark a progression of natural domains: heavens, earth, and mountains. The earth's fertility depends on God's ongoing creative activity, from the top down.

Verse 9 opens with a participle and concludes with a finite verb, similar to verses 2 and 5. In addition, the second colon is cast elliptically, despite the presence of a second verb. The opening verb ("give") is understood to apply to the second colon, thus governing the verse as a whole. The verse can be rendered prosodically as follows: A [a:b:c] / A′ [b′:d]. Despite its outwardly predictable structure, the verse does carry one syntactic distinction: because of its location in a subordinate clause (d), the second verb points not to God but to the object of God's providential care, the raven's brood. The reader's attention is thus drawn to the ravens' "cry," described in onomatopoeic fashion (*yiqrā'û*). Their cry is met by God's care.

Verses 10 and 11 conclude this strophe by highlighting the object of God's delight or favor. Breaking the participial syntax of earlier verses, verse 10 begins with a negative particle (*lō'*) in both cola and continues with identical syntactical sequencing, namely, object followed by verb. Prosodically, the verse exhibits straightforward, sequential parallelism: A [a:b:c] / A' [a':b':c']. It highlights two objects in which God does not find delight: equine strength and human legs. The latter reference stands for human speed. Together, the words evoke images of galloping horses and running warriors, both of which are rejected as objects of divine approbation.

The negative character of verse 10, however, paves the way for the positive pronouncement in verse 11, which identifies the true object of God's favor. Indeed, verse 11 picks up where verse 10 leaves off, namely, with the verb *rṣh*, denoting favor. This concluding verse is syntactically structured in similar fashion to verse 9, hence with nearly identical prosody: A [a:b:c] / A' [c':d]. Like the circumstantial clause of verse 9*b*, verse 11 also has its surprise ending. The second object is a participle whose subject is not divine but human, and the verse ends with the grammatical object of the participle, *ḥesed* ("benevolence"). The correspondences are revealing: God's favor extends to those who revere God and to those who place their hope in (or wait for) God's *ḥesed*. A more subtle correspondence is found between the object of reverence in the first colon, namely, God, and the object of hope in the second, God's *ḥesed*. As illustrated by the progressive parallelism, *ḥesed* defines most decisively God's character. On such an "exquisitely" conclusive note, the second strophe ends.

STROPHE III (VV. 12-20)

Laud, O Jerusalem, YHWH!
   Praise your God, O Zion!
For he has fortified the bars of your gates;
   he has blessed your children within you.
Who establishes your border with peace,
   and satisfies you with the finest wheat.
Who dispatches his command to the earth;
   swiftly runs his word.

He dispenses snow like wool;
  he scatters frost like ashes.
He hurls his ice like crumbs;
  before his cold who can stand?[51]
He sends forth his word and causes them to melt;
  he causes his wind to blow—waters flow.
He declares his word[52] to Jacob,
  his statutes and his judgments to Israel.
He has not done so with any other nation;
  as for (his) judgments, they do not know them.

The longest of the three strophes, this concluding section begins as the previous two, with opening imperatives of praise. However, this strophe does not make reference to music (cf. vv. 1, 7), and the opening commands are grammatically feminine and singular. These distinctions, as well as this stanza's overall length and thematic diversity, suggest the possibility that two originally separate psalms were conjoined.[53] Or perhaps this strophe's unique poetic qualities led the translators of the Old Greek text (or Septuagint) to mark this final section as a separate psalm.[54] The text-critical issue broaches a literary one, since it addresses the psalm's overall coherence (see below). For now, however, we note the fine poetic contours of each line of this final strophe before taking up the bigger poetic picture of the psalm as a whole.

Regarding the change in imperative voice in verse 12, the subjects of praise, cast in the vocative, are Jerusalem and Zion, here metaphorically conceived as female, as is common elsewhere in biblical tradition.[55] Note the reference to "children" in verse 13, suggesting a maternal image for the city in verse 12.[56] Structurally, verse 12 is tightly constructed in parallel fashion. The only change in word order is the transposition of the vocative and the object in the second colon (A [a:b:c] / A' [a':c':b']). The feminine address of verse 12 unites the subsequent two verses (vv. 13-14), which are characterized with the feminine second person suffix "your" in Hebrew (–ēk).

Verse 13 establishes its connection to the previous verse with the introductory conjunctive kî, as attested also in verse 1. Nevertheless, the function of this particle is markedly different in this context: it introduces the reason for the imperative of praise given in verse 12. The finite perfect verbs, appearing for the first time in the psalm, confirm the causal function of the clause.

Phonetically, alliteration characterizes this verse with the repeated final *kaphs* ("k"), denoting the feminine singular second-person suffix, as well as marking the ending of the verb "bless" (*bērak*). Indeed, the "k" phoneme is evident in every word but one in verse 13, giving the verse a staccato-like intonation. Semantically, the verbs "strengthened" and "blessed" are joined together, along with their respective objects, "bars of your gates" and "your children within you." The parallelism is neither synonymous nor antithetical but more loosely complementary (A [a:b:c:d] / A' [b':c':d']). In its separate cola, verse 13 denotes two different spatial perspectives: the gates within the city's walls and the children within the city, in keeping with the feminine figuration of the city in verse 12. The last phrase, in fact, can be translated: "he has blessed your children within your insides" (*běqirbēk*).[57] Zion's children flourish within the safety of her womb. Indeed, verse 13*a* can be understood in relation to the feminine image of the city that frames verses 12-14. Strengthened city gates have a good chance of preventing an invading army from penetrating the city's defenses, an act tantamount to rape. Poetically conceived, the city of Jerusalem is a female body.

Verse 14 resumes the typical hymnic opening with a substantive participle set in chiastic arrangement with a concluding finite verb (A [a:b:c] / A' [c':a':b']). Its close ties with the previous verse are clear. The feminine city remains the object of address ("your," – *ēk*), and the two cola complement each other spatially: secure borders from without and full sustenance from within. Peace and provision find their convergence in this verse. Or, to see it another way, the first colon in verses 13 and 14 refers to *constructed* forms of security, whereas the second colon in each verse introduces the *personal* dimension: "children" and "you," including the citizens of Zion.

Verses 15-20 mark the final section of the strophe (and of the psalm). This section describes the efficacy of God's "word," which is referenced in four different ways. God's "word" bears a multidimensional function that addresses both creation in general and Israel in particular (vv. 14, 18-19). Opening with the participle of praise, verse 15 conjoins "command" and "word" as interchangeable terms. But the syntax, and thus the prosody (A [a:b:c] / A' [d:a':b']), is varied in this verse, highlighting a significant shift in focus between "command" (the verbal object in the first colon) and "word" (the verbal subject in the second colon). The word choice is deliberate: God's "command" is sent by divine command. God's "word" takes on a life of its own, precisely in its fulfillment of being sent: it "runs swiftly." The medium is the messenger.

At first glance, the following two verses have little to do with God's "word." The language is rife with meteorological, rather than discursive, references: various forms of precipitation are featured in conjunction with various metaphors. Reflecting the syntax of praise in this psalm, verse 16 opens with a participle and concludes with a finite verb, and the "space" in between is filled with similes. Because the language of simile in Hebrew is typically introduced with the $k\breve{e}$ preposition, the ear is attuned to the word "frost" ($k\breve{e}p\hat{o}r$). The two cola are tightly linked by alliteration. Similarly, the second colon (v. 16b) is phonetically linked by the repetition of the letters pe and $resh$ (soft "p" and "r"): $k\breve{e}p\hat{o}r$ $k\bar{a}'\bar{e}per$ $y\breve{e}pazz\bar{e}r$. Prosodically, verse 16 reflects semichiastic ordering: A [a:b:c] / A'[b':c':a']. In keeping with the meteorological imagery, verse 17a describes ice as falling crumbs, as in the case of hail. The words "ice" ($qerah$) and "cold" ($q\bar{a}r\bar{a}h$) are phonetically similar as much as they are conceptually related and poetically paired. Verse 17, moreover, is prosodically more varied than verse 16: A [a:b:c] / A' [d:b':e]. Though concluding with a finite verb, the second colon of verse 17 disrupts the syntax by posing a rhetorical question: can anyone withstand the unbearable cold that comes from God's command?

Verses 16-17 burst with metaphorical images. Snow is likened to wool; frost is described as scattered ashes and hail as table scraps. On one level, the various similes highlight God's supreme power over the meteorological realm. One could continue the poet's metaphorical exuberance by likening, for example, the fearsome lightning bolts to, say, God's toothpicks. But there is also an undeniably aesthetic dimension to be discerned. The imagery of wool and ash suggests the common color of whiteness blanketing or dappling the ground (cf. Isa 1:18). There is something sublime about the wintry cold, the poet observes.

But what does all this have to do with God's "word"? Enter verse 18. Echoing verse 15, word is sent. The verb is cast not as a participle but as a finite imperfect verb to address the seasonal specificity described in verses 16-17. God's word breaks in and intervenes, and the parallelism of verse 18 testifies to its efficacy. Whereas verse 15 highlights the manner of God's word, namely, its swiftness, verse 18 vividly describes the effects of God's word: it melts the frozen precipitation. It is against the scene of unbearable cold (vv. 16-17) that God's "word" makes its entrance. In this case, God's word warms the world.

The parallelism of verse 18 is straightforward enough (A [a:b:c] / A'[a':b':c']), and yet subtleties abound. God remains the subject of both verbs in the first colon: God "sends his word" and God "melts" the frozen precipitation. In the second colon, the generic language of divine command (cf. v. 15a) is transformed into a more dynamic picture of divine breath or "wind" (rûaḥ). God's "word" is paired with God's warming wind, echoing perhaps the restless primordial scene in Gen 1:2. God remains subject: God "blows his breath/wind." But the flowing waters in their own right become the grammatical subject to conclude the verse: they "flow." This slight shift in the parallel structure of verse 18 highlights a grammatical ambiguity in the first colon. Is God the consistent subject in the first colon, or is God's "word" the subject of the second verb: "[God] sends forth his word, and it melts them"? In either case, God's "word" is instrumental in breaking the cold that grips the land.

In view of verses 15-17 as a whole, it seems that God's word, personified as a runner (v. 15b), also has a hand in producing the cold. Could the "word," rather than God, be the actual subject of the participles and finite verbs of verses 16-17? Grammatically, it is possible; however, the definite nature of the opening participle in verse 16 would count against it: "*the* one who dispenses snow" is likely God. And yet God's swiftly running "word" has a role in all that follows. Word and world are poetically bound. The character of the divine word is multifaceted: it takes an active role, yet at the same time recedes behind God's direct agency. The word sets the occasion for the meteorological events that unfold by divine decree and action. By pointing directly to divine activity, God's word is fully reified and thoroughly transparent.[58]

In the psalm's penultimate verse, God's "word" takes on additional nuance. In verse 19, the creative word becomes a word of polity, a constitutional word for Israel. This verse introduces both a different domain and a distinctive function for God's word. The setting is no longer the land in general and the world of weather but a particular people. And for this community, God's word functions uniquely. Syntactically, verse 19 opens with a participle that is extended elliptically into the second colon. Prosodically, the verse can be represented as A [a:b:c] / A' [b':c']. Most significant is the shift from (b) to (b'). The singular "word" is explicated as "statutes and judgments." The poetic pluralizing locates the divine word squarely in the realm of jurisprudence. The language of (b') thus evokes the language of *tôrâ* ("law"). The explication of God's "word" as "statutes" and "judgments" echoes the delineation of divine *tôrâ* as "decrees," "statutes," and "judgments" in Deut 4:44-45. The creative word that governs both weather and fertility is also Israel's constitutional word.

The final verse highlights Israel's distinctiveness in this regard. Framed by negated verbs, verse 20 breaks the parallel flow by shifting the grammatical subjects. The first colon builds on the previous verse: the statement "[God] has not done so" refers to God's unique imparting of Israel's constitutional word. The second colon is constructed grammatically as a *casus pendens,* or "hanging case," by which the first word serves also as the antecedent of the object suffix of the verbal clause ("them"). A prosodic mapping of verse 20 yields: A [a:b:c] / A' [b':a']. Segment (b), "so," refers back to the previous verse, as indicated above; (b'), "judgments," does the same. The shift from (a) to (a') is more significant, namely, the shift in subject from God to the nations. Each colon could be construed as the converse of the other: God has declared the word only to Israel and not to the other nations; hence, the nations do not know it. God's dissemination of this word is discriminating. This, too, as the final imperative claims, is cause for praise, but it is praise that only Israel can render. The nations are left out in the cold, as it were. The psalm, thus, concludes with the gift of God's unique word to Israel.

From Prosody to Perspective

Like its rich, prosodic "microworld," the psalm's overall perspective is both straightforward and subtle. Each strophe, in its own way, describes Israel's restoration and character within a broader, indeed cosmic, context. In strophe 1, God builds Jerusalem and names the stars. In strophe 2, God provides for all of nature and takes delight in those who demonstrate reverence. In strophe 3, God constitutes both weather and Israel, all by divine word.

Structurally, each strophe opens with either an affirmation of praise (v. 1) or a call to praise (vv. 7, 12), followed by an elucidation of the content of praise (vv. 2-6, 8-11, 13-20). Each covers both the cosmic and the communal. The first invokes God's unlimited power over the cosmos to declare God's ability to restore the exiles and the poor. God's naming of the stars (v. 4) reflects God's care for the exiles and the poor, each known by name. Indeed, the movement of the first strophe circles back on itself by correlating the "outcast" with the "poor." The second strophe lifts up God's providential care for all nature by providing rain for the land's fertility (specifically, "mountains") and, as a result, food for animals.

The second part of the strophe takes a surprising turn with its focus on God's special object of favor. The psalmist identifies those who revere and place their hope in God as the recipients of divine favor (v. 11). The claim is exquisitely cast: the imagery moves from cattle and ravens in verse 9, the objects of God's care, to horses and humans in verse 10—specifically their strength— the objects of God's nonfavor. Favor, rather, is given to those who fear and hope in God. The sublime movement of the second hymn, with its chain of natural images, holds in tension God's indiscriminate care for all life and God's discriminate favor for a few.

The final strophe also establishes some peculiar links. Opening with a call to mother Zion, this mini-hymn acknowledges the protection and care granted to Jerusalem's citizens (vv. 13-14). The first section concludes with the "satisfying" image of wholesome grain, emblematic of abundant sustenance (v. 14b). The surprising turn comes in the immediately following verses, which focus on God's efficacious word. As in the previous strophe, the focus shifts from the general, in this case meteorological phenomena, to the particular, namely, Israel's uniqueness. Within this movement, similes pile up on one another, and not simply for ornamental effect. At first glance, they are disorienting. God's precipitous word is dispatched as a speedy runner, highlighting the efficiency of God's command. The effect is snow, frost, and ice. The first two poetic images—"wool" and "ashes"—are cognitively dissonant in relation to what they designate. They connote warmth, not cold. Snow and frost, in effect, blanket the land. There is something salutary and beautiful, the poet subtly implies, about icy precipitation.

The third image, "crumbs," shifts the focus further. Most commonly associated with bread, "crumbs" are the meager remains of abundant provision. But hail—the metaphor's referent or target—is a destructive force. Hail is unbearably cold from the poet's perspective, but not so from a broader perspective—from that of the land and of God. Such is God's provision for the earth, to which the word is sent (v. 15a). God literally "gives (ntn) snow" (v. 16a), even though it is cold comfort to the earth's human inhabitants.

The various images of cold precipitated by God's word are incorporated into the language of provision, which extends well beyond human livelihood and concern. God's word is both cold and warm. The progression of images in verses 16-18, from the frozen to the flowing, inscribes God's word as seasonal, in sync with, perhaps even governing, the cycles of nature itself. God's word is not uniform or static; it is dynamic and efficacious! It is poetic. As God's word can change seasons, it can also change genres. The final part of the final strophe turns God's word from the creational to the constitutional, from the generally cosmic to the particularly communal (vv. 19-20). Although God's word is "declared" (v. 19a), taking on a peculiarly discursive form, it is incorporated into God's creative work: literally "God has not *made* it so with any other nation" (v. 20a).

God's constitutional word for Israel is folded into God's providential care. God's *tôrâ*, like God's warming, sustaining word for the land, provides. God's granting of *tôrâ* is testimony of God's sustaining care for Israel, as much as the finest of wheat, peaceful boundaries, and flourishing children testify to such care. The juxtaposition between God's constitutional word and God's "precipitous" word highlights, moreover, the multidimensional character of *tôrâ*, which, like precipitation, can be either cold or warm, harsh or life-giving. The psalmist rhetorically asks: who can stand before God's cold (v. 17)? Who, in turn, can stand before God's judgment (cf. Ps 1:5)? But *tôrâ* also sustains, like flowing streams and radiant sunlight (cf. Pss 1:2-3; 19:4b-13). The psalm acknowledges the shaping, creative power of God's word for Israel, a word that is equally claimed for the world.

Finally, a poetic wordplay in verses 9-10 vividly articulates God's favor. God is not impressed with human speed or equine strength. Instead, God's favor is oriented to those who fear God (regardless of how fast they can run). It is no coincidence, then, that the image of running is also used to describe God's word in verse 15. The swiftly running word overtakes, as it were, the human runner. The wordplay lies in the fact that the word "run" comes from the verbal root *ruṣ* and the word "favor" from the similar root *rṣh*. Such subtle links help establish the psalm's poetic coherence.

As for its overall coherence, the psalm is filled from beginning to end with the language of provision. As king and shepherd, God restores Jerusalem and community; as physician, God heals and binds wounds; as creator, God sets the stars in their courses; as judge and warrior, God restores the poor and overthrows the wicked; as sustainer, God provides rain and food, security and peace, the seasonal rhythm of cold and warmth, wet and dry. And finally as lawgiver, God grants *tôrâ* for Israel's guidance, indeed identity. In all these roles, God provides. The manifold nature of God's providential care is vividly expressed by the poet's evocative use of image and word, of movement and metaphor. Exquisite praise indeed!

CHAPTER 2

PSALMS AS POETRY: METAPHOR

O ur study of Psalm 147 in the previous chapter highlighted the intricacies of Hebrew prosody—the structured movement of poetic lines via parallel segments. Through its vivid use of imagery, the psalm, moreover, introduced us to the subtleties of metaphor. As noted earlier, the power of Hebrew poetry lies not only in its sonority and structure but also in its sensual power, particularly the power to evoke images. The Psalms, in particular, draw liberally from the rich iconography of the ancient world.[1] The verbal "icon," in short, is as essential to Hebrew psalmody as is parallelism.[2] According to Spanish exegete Luis Alonso Schökel, "Images are the glory, perhaps the essence of poetry, the enchanted planet of the imagination, a limitless galaxy, ever alive and ever changing."[3] Though perhaps too effusive in his description, Schökel rightfully advocates for a poetic analysis that involves discerning not only a psalm's verbal patterns but also its visual texture. Poetry weds sound and sense, including a visual sense.

The primary point of contact between the ancient text and the contemporary reader lies in what the psalm conjures in the reader's imagination through the imagery it employs. The psalm's impact on the reader is directly tied to the constellation of images, whose interconnections arrest the reader's attention.[4] As essential as parallelism is, Hebrew poetry would be incomplete without its amplifying, elucidating, startling images. "Like a blues song, [the Psalms] speak a vividly metaphorical language that is intensely personal and yet not private."[5] Indeed, it is the deployment of metaphor that lifts the ancient psalm beyond the confines of its specific context of usage and makes it available for readers of every age.

Handling Metaphors

What precisely, then, is a metaphor? In his *Rhetoric,* Aristotle marveled about its literary power: "Now strange words simply puzzle us; ordinary words convey only what we know already; it is from metaphor that we can best ascertain something fresh" (*Rhetoric* 1410^{b}12-14).[6] Since Aristotle, countless philosophers, literary theorists, and poets have attempted to discern how the metaphor produces "something fresh." In light of its Greek root, "metaphor" originally denoted the "carrying over" or "transference" of property (μετα ["trans"] and εφέζω ["carry"]). In the act of reading, metaphors facilitate the transference of meaning from something familiar to something new. Most modern definitions of metaphor include two elements that establish a correspondence or congruity. Janet Martin Soskice's definition is as good as any: "The metaphor is that figure of speech whereby we speak about one thing in terms [that] are seen to be suggestive of another."[7]

Every definition acknowledges at least two constitutive elements, the "one thing" and "another." How, precisely, to name these elements, and thereby indicate their interrelationship, has been the pressing challenge for every theorist. Best known are the labels given by I. A. Richards, namely, "tenor" and "vehicle," classifications that he admitted were "clumsy."[8] Studies of poetry, including biblical poetry, have been encumbered with the ambiguity of these terms. The "tenor" is the "underlying idea," "principal subject," or conceptual meaning signified. The "vehicle" is the mode or figure by which the "tenor" is expressed.[9] Other concerted attempts at naming these two components include Max Black's distinction between "the 'primary' subject and the 'secondary' one,"[10] and the recent designations given by Paul Avis, "occasion" and "image."[11] Unexplained among all these classifications, however, is a precise accounting of how these two components of metaphor relate to each other in a particular context.

To fill this gap, cognitive literary theorists George Lakoff and Mark Turner have attempted to describe more precisely how metaphors work, not just in poetic language but also in everyday speech and rational discourse. Like their predecessors, they distinguish two essential components; their innovation lies in identifying how they are related. Taking the example of the metaphor "time is a thief," Lakoff and Turner describe how the two parts are related:

> We use a metaphor to map certain aspects of the *source domain* onto the *target domain,* thereby producing a *new understanding* of that target domain. In this case, part of that mapping *superimposes* a metaphorical understanding of youth as a possession, which carries with it our normal feelings about possessions—that we have a right to keep them and that it would be unjust for them to be taken away.[12]

The terms "target domain" and "source domain" not only acknowledge a certain parity of importance between the metaphor and its referent, but they also illustrate more precisely what happens when something is referenced metaphorically—a superimposing or unilateral "mapping" of one domain upon another.[13] Such "transference" of meaning results in a new understanding of the target domain (in this case, time) but not necessarily of the source domain (theft and possessions).[14] Through the use of metaphor, "time" is understood or perceived differently. Nothing new, however, is said of possessions or thieves. To take a biblical example, the psalmist's statement that "YHWH God is a sun and shield" (Ps 84:12) highlights the (royal) efficacy of divine blessing but, by itself, no more implies solar worship than it suggests the veneration of shields. The source domain illuminates a new, crucial dimension of its target (God), but the reverse does not apply.

Thus, according to Lakoff and Turner, "Metaphorical understanding is not a matter of mere wordplay; it is endemically conceptual in nature."[15] For the metaphor to work, an understanding of both domains must be gained before new insight is achieved. There must be a recognizable correspondence between the metaphor and its target domain that can be acknowledged by both poet and reader, otherwise the metaphor remains indecipherable. Lakoff and Turner offer the example "death is a banana," a metaphor devoid of sense, an example of *catachresis,* or the improper use of metaphor.[16] The true and effective metaphor, by contrast, stands on the ground of shared knowledge and builds on that knowledge in a way that elicits new inferences and connections.

On the one hand, if a metaphor is too enigmatic, it only "puzzles" the reader like "strange words," to quote Aristotle. On the other hand, a metaphor that is too obvious or conventional packs no punch. It leads to no new understanding, no real transference of meaning. Such metaphors are fully lexicalized and literal.[17] They are "dead." The "dead metaphor" is devoid of figurative connections. In a "living metaphor," however, "there is dissonance or tension...whereby the terms of the utterance used seem not strictly appropriate to the topic at hand."[18] A banal metaphor, by contrast, exhibits so much similarity or near equivalency between its source and target as to be superfluous or mechanical. A good metaphor thus effectively weds analogy and anomaly;[19] it creates conceptual and emotional friction by which new meaning is achieved and, in the words of Aristotle, "something fresh" is ascertained. The creative metaphor is a master of surprise but not a source of puzzlement.

To summarize, a metaphor in a given context does not so much *fuse* together two or more modes of perception as *superimpose* one upon another, specifically a source domain onto its target domain. Such mapping generates a new understanding of the target, enabling "one to see similarities in what previously had been regarded as dissimilars."[20] Put more precisely, the metaphor acts, in effect, as a grid or filter that enables the reader to see something new about the target domain and thereby gain new insight about the metaphor's object.

An effective metaphor navigates between two extremes. It avoids, on the one hand, recycling obvious or overly conventional connections between the source and the target; on the other hand, it refrains from establishing connections that are conceptually incompatible. A metaphor is in the business of generating a "new vision, the birth of a new understanding, a new referential access. A strong metaphor compels new possibilities of vision."[21]

As essential as both are to Hebrew poetry, metaphor and parallelism actually share some common ground. Both involve the transference of meaning. As noted in the previous chapter, parallelism involves the transference of perception in the process of "semantic modification," to quote Viktor Shklovsky.[22] In the case of Hebrew poetry, meaning conveyed in the first colon is invariably modified in the subsequent colon or cola. Something of the same can be said of metaphor. In the act of reading, metaphors facilitate the transference of meaning from something familiar to something new, but the end result does not necessarily lead to semantic precision. A metaphor's contribution to the construction of meaning is more suggestive than propositional, more generative than limiting. Indeed, with any literary image, metaphorical or not, there is a "natural polyvalency" that "resists reduction to propositional summation."[23] Such is the way of poetry. Through metaphor, poetry generates a surplus of semantic connections.

Of Shepherds and Shadows: Psalm 23

As a prosodic analysis "maps" the dynamic, verbal structure of a poetic line, so a metaphorical analysis helps "map" the images and their significance within a given psalm. One striking example is found in Psalm 23.

A Psalm of David
YHWH is my shepherd;
   I lack nothing.
In meadows of grass he lets me lie;
   to waters of repose he leads me,
      refreshing my soul.
On account of his name,
   he leads me on paths of righteousness.[24]
Even as I sojourn in the darkest valley,
   I fear no danger,
for you are with me;
   your rod and your staff—they give me comfort.
You arrange before me a table before my enemies.
   You anoint my head with oil;
      my cup is well filled.
Only[25] goodness and kindness shall pursue[26] me
   all the days of my life,

so that may I dwell[27] in the house of YHWH
  as long as I live.

The psalm is well known for its host of evocative images: shepherd, grass, meadows, still waters, path, dark valley, rod and staff, table, cup, and oil. Drawn from various source domains, together they give the psalm its distinctive coherence and movement.

The Good Shepherd

The psalm opens with images drawn from the pastoral domain: with God as shepherd, the speaker enjoys the security of rest in grassy meadows and the provision of still waters. An exploration of the shepherd metaphor, particularly in light of its background outside of Psalm 23, yields a fuller picture of the metaphor's function within the psalm. This metaphor, in fact, has deep roots in biblical and ancient Near Eastern literature that fill out not only its source domain but also its target. For example, in his famous law code, Hammurabi, the first ruler of the Babylonian Empire (ca. 1728–1686 B.C.E.), proclaimed himself not only as "the pious prince" (*rubûm na'dum*) and "king of justice" (*šar mīšarim*) but also as "shepherd of the people" (*rē'î nišî*).[28] His epilogue develops the metaphor further:

> I made the people of all settlements lie in safe pastures, I did not tolerate anyone intimidating them. The great gods having chosen me, I am indeed the shepherd who brings peace, whose staff is just. My benevolent shadow is spread over my city, I held the people of the lands of Sumer and Akkad safely on my lap. They prospered under my protective spirit, I maintained them in peace, with my skillful wisdom I sheltered them.[29]

As the good shepherd and "benevolent shadow," Hammurabi boasts of his generous provision for his subjects, granting them rest and peace, prosperity and protection—not unlike what the speaker says of God in Psalm 23. Hammurabi's "staff is just," literally "straight." It is his scepter. Similarly, YHWH's "staff" provides comfort and peace. The shepherd metaphor thus serves to turn the privileged and powerful office of king into a responsibility of tender care.

Elsewhere in biblical literature, the shepherd metaphor frequently designates a position of leadership, particularly that of king.[30] David is considered the exemplary royal shepherd, as affirmed in God's message to David through the prophet Nathan:

> Wherever I moved about with all the Israelites, did I ever say to any of Israel's tribal leaders, whom I charged to shepherd my people Israel, saying, "Why have you not built me a house made out of cedar?" Now...thus you shall say to David my servant: "Thus says YHWH of hosts: I took you from the pasture, from following the flock to be ruler over my people Israel." (2 Sam 7:7-8)

According to Nathan's oracle, the "tribal leaders" had the responsibility of "shepherding" Israel, that is, governing God's people. But now is the time for David, the erstwhile shepherd boy, to "be ruler over" Israel. A tighter connection between shepherding sheep and ruling a nation is found in Psalm 78:

> He chose David, his servant,
>   taking him from the sheepfolds.
> He brought him from the ewes,
>   to shepherd Jacob his people
>   and Israel his inheritance.
> He shepherded them with the integrity[31] of his heart;
>   with the skillfulness of his hands he led them. (vv. 70-72)

The passage plays on David's former occupation as qualification and, indeed, standard for the royal office. To shepherd is to rule with care and guidance.

The shepherding role, of course, is not limited to earthly kings, Davidic or otherwise. As in Psalm 23, God takes on the role of shepherd in Ezekiel:

> I myself will shepherd my flock, and I will make them lie down, says the Lord YHWH. The lost I will seek, the strayed I will bring back, the injured I will bind up, and the weak I will strengthen. But the fat and the strong I will destroy. I will shepherd them with justice. (Ezek 34:15-16)

Such are the various responsibilities that the divine shepherd resolves to fulfill. Serving as the source domain for the metaphor, the pastoral imagery works well throughout the list until we come to the last two items, where it meets its limit. Unlike a human shepherd, the divine shepherd in Ezekiel will cull out the choice sheep for the sake of the injured and the weak! The last item on the list, moreover, reveals the true target of the shepherd metaphor: the divine king. God's provision is not, literally, rich pasturage, as sheep would want, but "justice." Drawn from the pastoral domain and applied to the domain of divine kingship, the shepherd metaphor vividly highlights God's intention to protect and provide for the weakest of the "flock."

The metaphor of the divine shepherd is by no means confined to Psalm 23. It appears in several other psalms.

> YHWH is strength for his people;[32]
>> he is a saving refuge for his anointed.
> Save your people, and bless your heritage;
>> shepherd them and carry them forever. (28:8-9)

> O Shepherd of Israel, listen up,
>> you who lead Joseph like sheep! (80:1)

> Know that YHWH *is* God—
>> it is he who made us and not we ourselves;[33]
>>> his people (we are), the sheep of his pasture. (100:3)

In these passages, the shepherding image is associated with salvation, blessing, governance, and protection. All these nuances come to bear in Psalm 23 to reveal the sovereign behind the shepherd.

From Pasture to Sanctuary

In consort with the shepherd imagery, the idyllic images that populate the first verses of Psalm 23 "map out" God's royal protection and guidance. In contrast to the secure path, the valley of darkness evokes an element of danger (v. 4*a*), highlighting all the more God's protective role as shepherd. In verse 5, however, the scene shifts from the pastoral to the domestic: the images of table, oil, and cup point to God's abundant provision and hospitality. No longer shepherd, God is now gracious host. With enemies held at bay and the speaker seated at the table, protection and provision are served. Finally, the domestic turns sacred, as the speaker proclaims a desire to dwell in YHWH's "house." As a whole, the psalm's movement is governed by dramatic shifts in source domains—from pasture to home to sanctuary—all to underscore the speaker's testimony of provision and protection.

34

More remarkable still is the surprising metaphorical turn taken in the final verse, in which declaration is made that God's "goodness and kindness (*ṭôb wāḥesed*) will *pursue*" the speaker. The verb itself suggests persecution, specifically of enemies stalking and persecuting the speaker (cf. vv. 4*a*, 5*b*). But as the table scene makes clear, the threat posed by the speaker's unnamed enemies is no more. Now there is another "threat." The source domain of persecution is mapped onto the target domain of divine benevolence. The result is an ironic, not to mention riveting, transformation: God's benevolence takes on an aggressive quality. The metaphor of pursuit, as applied to God, effectively displaces the role that the enemies once had. The speaker joyously declares being the target not of enemies but of God's love, from which there is no escape. In dogged pursuit, God's benevolence will track down to secure and bless the speaker. The hunt is on—a hunt that the speaker fully welcomes!

Thirsty for God: Psalm 42:1-8

Sometimes a single source domain in a given psalm will cover or map a variety of target domains. Take, for example, the opening verses of Psalm 42.[34]

> As a doe[35] longs for ravines of water,
>> so my soul longs for you, O God.
> My soul thirsts for God, the living God.
>> When shall I come and see[36] the face of God?
> My tears have been my food day and night,
>> while it is said[37] to me all day, "Where is your God?"
> These things I remember as I pour out my soul within me:
>> How I passed through to the abode of the Mighty One,[38]
>>> to the house of God,
>> with cries of joy and thanksgiving,
>>> a multitude making festival.
> Why so downcast, O my soul,
>> and why so clamorous within me?[39]
> Hope in God; for I shall yet give thanks to him,
>> my saving presence and my God.[40]
> My soul is downcast within me;
>> no wonder[41] I remember you from the land of
>>> Jordan and Hermon, from Mount Mizar.[42]

Deep calls to deep at the noise of your cascades;
    all your breakers and your billows pass over me.
By day YHWH commands his benevolence,
    and by night his song is with me,
        praise[43] to the God of my life.

Water imagery flows mightily through the first seven verses, spilling from the first stanza into the second (vv. 1-5 and 6-11). As the first verse introduces the thirsty deer searching for flowing ravines, water imagery concludes with a vivid scene of inundation in verse 7. The first seven verses thus begin with too little water and conclude with ostensibly too much. In between, the desiccation and the deluge are two interlocking memories that rise to the discursive surface.

The opening imagery is cast as an extended simile. Drawn from a stock of faunal images,[44] the doe designates the "soul" (*nepheš*), a self-referential term comparable to the English "I" in its most self-disclosive form. By the same metaphorical token, the deer's object of desire, "water," points to God. God is likened to water that quenches the thirsty *nepheš*. An analogy is born: as much as a doe yearns for water, so the speaker longs for God. At the point of dehydration, metaphorically speaking, the speaker feels godforsaken.

The images of "doe" and "flowing ravines," moreover, share a common domain. They are both drawn from the setting of the wilderness, and it is within this landscape that the poet initially frames the speaker's relationship with God. Further background about this metaphorical schema sheds light on the poet's view of God. Ravines or wadis in Palestine are not perennial streams: they flow, dry up, and flow again, all depending on the amount of fallen rainwater. There are two main seasons in the Middle East: a warm, dry summer and a cool, wet winter. The sudden downpours associated with late fall and winter are precisely what is required for filling ravines.

The poet draws from the episodic nature of flowing ravines to describe the sporadic relationship between God and the speaker: the speaker searches for God's sustaining presence but to no avail, hence the plaintive question posed in verse 2b. The speaker is experiencing the "drought" of God's absence. Flowing streams morph into shed tears; thirst turns into grief (v. 3). The speaker is on the verge of dissolution. In just three verses, the role of water has changed from a source of sustenance, indicating God's presence, to a sign of sorrow. In God's absence, water becomes the medium of grief; tears shed are the metonym of sorrow. But there is more: in grief, the speaker "pours out" his or her soul in a kenotic act of self-disclosure (v. 4*a*). Now the soul itself, the speaker's personal identity, is a body of water poured out before God, but not in an act of self-emptying dissolution, as the imagery alone might suggest. This act of pouring, it turns out, is an act of self-survival.

When Memory Is Hope

The speaker pours out his or her soul before God by recalling two vivid memories of God's presence: of Israel at worship in the temple (42:4) and of nature at "worship" near Hermon (vv. 6-7). The first memory recalls the audible marks of temple worship, the overwhelming "surround sound" of praise generated by "cries of joy and thanksgiving" (*qôl rinnâ wĕtôdâ*). The speaker longingly recalls the clamor of festive worship within God's sanctuary. The vivid word *hāmôn* ("multitude") in verse 4*b* conveys a tumultuous scene of sight and sound. The semantic range of this evocative term, however, extends well beyond the setting of worship. The term can refer to the powerful resonance of billowing waves (Jer 51:42),[45] sea (Isa 60:5; Ps 65:8), rain (1 Kgs 18:41), and water (Jer 10:13; 51:16), as well as designate the inner groanings of the self, which the speaker describes in the following refrain by use of its verbal root in verse 5 (*hmh*). The speaker recalls an experience of total immersion in worship.

The second memory is more ambiguous but just as evocative. Far removed from the temple setting, God's presence is felt at the headwaters of the Jordan. Geographically, the Jordan River gushes from the foot of Hermon in northern Palestine. Towering above the Biqa' valley at 9,232 feet above sea level, Hermon is snowcapped most of the year. (One of its Arabic names is Jabal al-Thalj, "the snow mountain.") Like a sponge, this large, convex block of limestone soaks up the melting snow, thereby providing at its base water for the Jordan in the form of spectacular waterfalls. There, the speaker hears the roar of cascading, turbulent waters, and is figuratively swept away. The speaker finds the voice of the deep powerfully liturgical (42:7*a*). For this thirsty "doe," the floodgates are now opened. No still waters here. God, it turns out, is no babbling brook. The speaker thus recalls two places of being overwhelmed with God's presence: in the temple and in the wilderness.

From Chaos to Choir

The interlocking of these two memories establishes a mutual interaction in this psalm. The "surround sound" of temple worship and the enveloping roar of mighty waters find common resonance, and therein lies the metaphorical surprise. Set by itself, the roar of the "deep" in verse 7 suggests a scene of "chaos and death."[46] But set in its larger metaphorical context, this ostensibly horrifying scene shares in the divine *mysterium tremendum*. It conveys something of God's awe-filled presence, a presence also felt in the temple. The source domain of turbulent waters flows into temple worship, imbuing it with a touch of the chaotic. Reciprocally, the memory of clamorous worship invests the chaotic din of the depths with profound liturgical nuance. "Deep calls to deep" reverberates with antiphonal praise. Like the cries of joy and praise that accompanied the speaker within the temple walls, so the speaker is surrounded by the roar and crash of cascading waters.

As the speaker was once engulfed in worship, so the "breakers" and "billows" of the Jordan engulf the speaker in thunderous discourse. Cascading waters find their parallel with the "multitude making festival." The "breakers" and "billows" resonate with the thunderous sounds of "joy" and "thanksgiving" echoing off temple walls. They resound in responsive worship, and the speaker is awestruck. The scene need not be read so literally as to "reflect the physical torture of someone who has been thrown or has fallen into a mountain torrent, whose billows have tossed him from rock to rock."[47] The scene is metaphorical. The speaker is submerged in nature at worship, just as he or she was immersed in temple worship. So what does nature proclaim in worship? Perhaps, as Klaus Seybold suggests, it is related to verse 8, which the psalmist casts hymnically.[48] For the speaker, deep to deep proclaims YHWH's benevolence and praise, all day and all night, like perennially cascading waterfalls.

In sum, the waters that issue forth from the foothills of Hermon and resound throughout upper Jordan's watersheds point to the *mysterium tremendum* of God, an overpowering experience of the divine that prompts utter awe. The scene that unfolds in verse 8 is not one of stark chaos endangering the speaker with mighty waves that represent the speaker's enemies,[49] but of nature at worship, engulfing the speaker in praise. No literal fear of drowning is registered here; there is no prayer for rescue. The speaker finds the voice of the deep powerfully liturgical, not life-threatening. If the mighty torrents can clap their hands, if the seas can thunder in joy (98:7-8) and the deeps render praise to God (148:7) elsewhere in the Psalter, then why not here? The author of Psalm 42 has shown through the evocative use of metaphor just such a transformation, from chaos to choir.

Beyond Poetry

Metaphor and prosody, the visual and the verbal, are the two poles of poetry. And within these two poles, the Psalms offer a veritable treasure trove of poetic gems, whether it is the subtle coordination of parallel segments or the transference of conventional images into new metaphorical domains, all dynamically interrelated. Together, image and sound reveal something of the Psalms' microworld in which the construction and transformation of meaning is at work. But the Psalms are, of course, more than simply nuggets of parallel segments and interconnected images. Each psalm bears its own larger coherence, one that exhibits both structure and movement. Some psalms exhibit typical form; others break the mold. But all have their integrity, literary and rhetorical. Hence, our next focus of study: from the poetic to the generic contours of individual psalms. As we did at the conclusion of our study of Psalm 147 in the first chapter, such a move involves stepping back from examining individual poetic lines to viewing individual psalms as whole entities, as networks of movement and meaning. But in doing so, may we never lose sight of the little elements and subtle relationships that make the Psalms what they are at the most fundamental level: poetry.

CHAPTER 3

PSALMS AS SPECIES

Like snowflakes, no two psalms are entirely alike.[1] Nevertheless, most exhibit common forms or patterns. Delineating them has been a staple of psalms study for more than a century, and it always will be, for identifying distinctive patterns stems from a basic human proclivity to name and classify things according to their similarities and differences, whether animal, vegetable, or mineral. Or psalms. Call it the taxonomic impulse. Classifying psalms by form, function, or some other aspect seems to be reflected in a number of the psalmic super-scriptions or titles, though the precise meaning behind some of them remains elusive: "*miktām*" (16, 56–59, 60), "*maśkîl*" (32, 42–44, 52–55, 74, 142), "prayer" (17, 90, 102, 142), "praise," (145), "song" (46, 48, 65–68, 75, 76, 108), "love song" (45), and "thanks-giving" (100).

Psalmic Genres

Since the groundbreaking work of Hermann Gunkel (1862–1932), the father of "form-criticism," biblical scholars have

41

identified various types of psalms, not unlike field biologists who classify botanical species in the tradition of Carolus Linnaeus (1707–1778), the father of modern taxonomy. The basic presupposition of form-criticism is that any given psalm is best understood not in isolation but in relation to its larger literary and social context, specifically in relation to psalms of similar type and implied usage. Each type, Gunkel argued, is characterized by common structure, shared language, similar content, and common "setting in life" (*Sitz im Leben*). All these characteristics together constitute a psalm's genre (*Gattung*). Among the 150 psalms of the Psalter, Gunkel identified five major types:[2]

> Hymns
> Communal Complaint Songs
> Royal Psalms
> Individual Complaint Songs
> Individual Thanksgiving Songs

In addition, Gunkel identified several subtypes, among them the pilgrimage song, victory song, and communal thanksgiving song.[3] Mixed types, he noted, are also not uncommon in the Psalter.

To press a modern analogy, genres are akin to "fuzzy sets" in mathematics, in which the delineation of types are far from distinct. They can only be drawn approximately, allowing for overlapping anatomical features. Those features include at least three related aspects: (1) the psalm's formal components; (2) the interrelationship of those components; and (3) the overall shape or *Gestalt* of the psalm. All three of these aspects figure in the identification of an individual psalm's anatomy, and from psalms that share similar anatomy a genre is born. Put simply, the quest for a genre, somewhat like identifying a species, highlights a psalm's typicality in relation to other psalms. It attempts to establish "family resemblances" among psalms, whether they are cousins or siblings.

Identifying the genre of a psalm, however, carries certain liabilities. It was once thought that the form of a particular psalm directly reflected its setting in life or *Sitz im Leben,* that is, its institutional context of usage (e.g., cultic setting, educational setting, family setting, etc.). Recent scholarship, however, has shown no tight correspondence between a psalm's form and its alleged setting. Psalms of similar structure and common language can reflect different contexts of usage, from public worship to individual devotion. A psalm's functional setting, in other words, is a moving target.

Another liability is the temptation to overlook what makes a particular psalm distinctive, even unique. Genre analysis by itself can make psalms appear, well, generic. Still, such study is quite useful. A genre conveys a set of expectations that helps the reader identify and anticipate how a particular psalm moves from beginning to end, or how it *could have* moved. Serving as a sort of template, a genre can also reveal how a particular psalm tweaks the common pattern, thereby highlighting its distinctiveness within the family of psalms with which it shares certain features. In the taxonomic task, identity and individuality are intimately connected.

But first identity. The following discussion treats three major genres exemplified in the Psalter: the complaint (or "lament"), the hymn or song of praise, and the thanksgiving psalm. Each type exhibits shared constituent parts and a common literary pattern. We will sample the psalms that fit the form almost to a T and identify a few that appear to break the mold in certain ways. As one would expect, there are certain psalms that do not correspond to any set pattern, although they can still be classified according to common theme, context, or style. These too will be noted.

Complaint Psalms

Variously called laments, complaints, prayers for help, or petitions, this category comprises the largest group of psalms in the Bible, more than one-third of the Psalter. Indeed, they form the Psalter's "backbone." Generically, they are most frequently cast in the first-person singular voice ("I"). A simple, paradigmatic example of the individual complaint psalm (Gunkel's "individual lament") is Psalm 13, translated below:

> To the director. A Psalm of David.
> How long, YHWH, will you forget me? Forever?[4]
>   How long will you hide your face from me?
> How long must I bear counsels[5] within my soul,
>   sorrow in my heart daily?
>   How often must my enemy rise up against me?
> Take note (and) answer me, YHWH, my God!

Restore light to my eyes,
  lest I fall into the sleep of death,
lest my enemy say, "I have overpowered him,"
  and my foes rejoice over my downfall.[6]
But as for me, I trust in your benevolence (*ḥesed*).
  My heart shall indeed rejoice in your salvation.
I will sing to YHWH,
  when[7] he has dealt fully[8] with me.

What makes this psalm an individual complaint or petition are its constitutive parts and overall structure. One can discern the main components that constitute the psalm's anatomy: invocation (v. 1), complaint (vv. 1-2), petition (vv. 3-4), and affirmation of trust and praise (v. 5), all presented in a rhetorically deliberate order. The complaint is cast as a series of questions that opens with an invocation. It describes the speaker's lamentable state: he or she feels abandoned by God, bears inner "sorrow," and suffers from social hostility (v. 2). The complaint, however, does not stand on its own but serves to introduce the petition that follows in which God is called upon to restore the speaker's life. An added feature to the petition is the motivation the speaker articulates to compel God to act (vv. 3*b*, 4*a*). If God fails to act, then the speaker will die, and his or her enemies will exult in triumph. God will, in effect, have one less person to render praise, and the speaker's enemies will have all the more reason to flout their arrogance. The speaker makes the case, none to subtly, that God's reputation is at stake. Completing its movement, the psalm concludes with an affirmation of trust and a vow to praise.

The pattern of this kind of psalm, as with all forms in the Psalter, is typical but not uniformly applicable. One exceptional example is Psalm 88, which does not conclude with praise or affirmation of trust but remains stuck in complaint to the bitter end.

A Song. A Psalm of the Korahites. To the leader according to *mahalat leannoth*. A *maśkîl* of Heman the Ezrahite.
YHWH, God of my salvation;
  by day I cry out,
    at night (I am) before you:
May my prayer come before you;
  incline your ear to my loud cry.
For my soul is sated with distress,

and my life has reached Sheol.
I am reckoned with those descending to the Pit;
    I am like a strongman bereft of help.
Among the dead (I am) free,
    like the slain, lying in the grave,
whom you no longer remember,
    cut off they are by your hand.
You have set me in the nethermost parts of the Pit,
    in dark places, in the depths.
Your wrath lies upon me,
    and with all your breakers you afflict (me). *Selah*
You have distanced my intimates from me;
    you have set me up as an abomination to them.
        Constrained, I cannot escape.
My eye tires from my affliction.
    I have called to you, YHWH, all day long;
        I have spread out my hands to you.
Do you work wonders for the dead?
    Do the shades[9] rise up and give you thanks? *Selah*
Is your benevolence declared in the grave,
    your faithfulness in *Abaddon*?[10]
Are your wonders known in the darkness,
    and your righteousness in the land of oblivion?
But I cry out to you, YHWH;
    let my prayer greet you in the morning.
Why do you, YHWH, spurn my soul?
    (Why) do you hide your face from me?
Afflicted I am and have been near death since youth;
    I have endured your terrors only to become lifeless.[11]
Your fiery wrath has swept over me;
    your terrors have struck me dumb.
They surround me like waters all day long;
    they engulf me altogether.
You have distanced friend and neighbor from me;
    darkness is my friend.[12]

Contrary to most complaint or petition psalms, Psalm 88 never resolves itself. Any affirmation of trust or ringing cry of praise is far from this speaker's mouth. Moreover, there is not even much petition present: only verses 2 and 13 adopt the posture of petition, but merely in passing. In fact, the typical order is reversed in this psalm:

45

in both cases, petition (little that there is) *precedes* complaint. In this psalm, complaint overwhelms petition, displacing it from its normal position and stripping it of all specific content. For the most part, the speaker's fist, rather than open hand, is raised to God.

An examination of the psalm's structure reveals that Psalm 88 actually consists of two extensive complaints, as the outline below illustrates:

I. Complaint 1	vv. 1-9*a*
A. Invocation and prayer	v. 1*a*
B. Prayer and petition	vv. 1*b*-2
C. Complaint	vv. 3-9
1. Death	vv. 3-6
2. God's wrath	v. 7
3. Social isolation	v. 8
4. Fatigue	v. 9*a*
II. Complaint 2	vv. 9*b*-18
A. Report of psalmist's praying	v. 9*b*
B. Rhetorical questions	vv. 10-12
C. Petition	v. 13
D. Complaint	vv. 14-18
1. Questions	v. 14
2. Speaker's condition	vv. 15-18
a. God's terrors	vv. 15-17
b. Social isolation	v. 18

Though separated in the middle of verse 9, both complaints are intimately related. Their respective endings, for example, convey wrenching alienation and isolation. Of all the psalms, this one comes closest to entering the dark, encompassing realm of death, where the speaker is cut off from friends and God. In Sheol, the speaker asserts, praise is an impossibility. Psalm 88 is the Psalter's most agonizing complaint. It is pure lament.

Similar to the individual complaints are the "communal complaints," or prayers whereby the corporate voice of the community rather than that of the individual is articulated. These psalms frequently lament God's abandonment and recall God's saving work in the past. A prime example is Psalm 79.

A Psalm. Of Asaph.
O God, the nations have come upon your inheritance;

46

they have defiled your holy temple;
 they have laid Jerusalem in ruins.
They have given your servants' corpses as food for the birds
  of the air,
 the flesh of your faithful to the wild animals of the earth.
They have spilled their blood like water,
 all around Jerusalem with none to bury (them).
We have become an insult to our neighbors,
 scorn and contempt to those around us.
How long, YHWH, will you rage? Forever?
 Will your anger burn like fire?
Pour out your wrath upon the nations,
 who refuse to acknowledge you.
And on the kingdoms,
 which have not called upon your name.
For they have devoured Jacob,
 and laid waste his abode.
Do not remember against the iniquity of earlier times;
 let your compassion quickly meet us,
  for we are brought very low.
Help us, O God of our salvation;
 for the glory of your name.
Deliver us and cover our sins,
 for the sake of your name.
Why should the nations say,
 "Where is their God?"
Let the avenging of the outpoured blood of your servants
 be known among the nations before our eyes.
Let the groaning of the prisoner come before you;
 by your powerful arm spare those destined for death.
And give back to our neighbors sevenfold, into their very
  bosom,
 the insults with which they insulted you, O Lord.
We are, after all, your people and the sheep of your pasture.
 We will give thanks to you forever;
  from generation to generation we will proclaim your
  praises.

Like the typical individual complaint psalms, this communal psalm proceeds from complaint (vv. 1-5) to petition (vv. 6-12), and concludes with an expression of praise (v. 13). The initial

47

complaint graphically describes Jerusalem's destruction, desecration, and international derision. The petition, which constitutes the bulk of the psalm, calls upon God to punish the nations and deliver "Jacob" (Israel). Reasons are given: the nations have violated Israel (v. 7), Israel's desolation provides occasion for the nations to gloat (v. 10a), God's reputation is at stake (vv. 9-10a), Israel enjoys a special relationship with God (v. 13a), and the community promises to render praise (v. 13b).

Nevertheless, as with certain individual complaint psalms, several communal prayers do not conform to this seemingly set pattern. Both Psalms 44 and 89, for example, do not resound in praise at their conclusion but remain either in complaint or petition. Indeed, the first half of each psalm sets up the conditions for praise (44:1-9; 89:1-37) only to be deconstructed in the second half (44:9-22; 89:38-51). While Psalm 44 ends with petition (vv. 23-26), Psalm 89 remains mired in complaint, much like its individual counterpart Psalm 88.

Examining the typical psalms of this genre, along with some notable exceptions, reveals how this genre reflects a spectrum that spans, at one end, the complaint or lament and, at the other end, the petition and praise. Most psalms in this category cover both ends, but in varying degrees. Perhaps the best way to designate this flexible genre is "complaint-petition," a generic label with a built-in acknowledgement of its range of form. Depending on their structures, some psalms fall more on the side of complaint (e.g., 22:1-21; 38; 80; 88), while others feature the petition more prominently (e.g., 5, 6, 7, 20, 26, 83). Others give nearly equal attention to both (e.g., 13). But it is rarely the case that a psalm of this genre is *either* a complaint or a petition, since both generic components are typically present.

In light of the spectrum this genre represents, one of the great enigmas of "complaint-petition" psalms, whether individual or communal, is their frequent but abrupt shifts from complaint and petition, on the one hand, to trust and praise, on the other (excluding, e.g., 39 and 88). Psalm 13, discussed previously, indicates such a move from verse 4 to verse 5, from complaining about strong enemies to trusting in God's benevolence. No ostensible reason, however, is given to account for this change, no explanation as to what triggers the shift. Simply put, "shift happens," and it does so suddenly and without warning. This puzzling matter takes us to perhaps the most elaborate and certainly most well known complaint-petition psalm in the Psalter, Psalm 22.

To the director, according to the "Doe of the Dawn."
A Psalm of David.
My God, my God, why have you forsaken me?
    (Why) so far from my cry,[15] the words of my screaming?
My God, I cry out by day, but you do not answer;
    at night I have no relief.
Yet you are holy,
    enthroned on the praises of Israel.
In you our ancestors placed their trust.
    They trusted and you delivered them.
To you they cried, and they escaped;
    in you they trusted, and they were not put to shame.
But I am a worm, and not human,
    an object of human reproach and despised by people.
All who see me deride me;
    they open up (their) lips;
        they shake their heads.
"He has committed himself[14] to YHWH; let him deliver him.
    Let him save him, for he delights in him."
But it was you who pulled me out of the womb,
    keeping me safe upon my mother's breasts.
Upon you I was cast at birth,
    from my mother's womb you have been my God.
Do not be far from me,
    for distress is near,
        for there is no one to help.
Many bulls encompass me;
    the mighty ones of Bashan surround me.
They open wide their mouths at me,
    a lion tearing and roaring.
Like water I am poured out;
    all my bones have fallen apart.
My heart has become like wax;
    it has melted within me.
My strength[15] is dried up like a shard;
    and my tongue is stuck to my jaw;
        and in the dust of death you set me.
For dogs surround me; a pack of evildoers encompass me.

Like a lion … my hands and my feet.[16]
I take count of all my bones;
    while they gaze and gloat over me.
They divide up my garments among them,
    and for my clothing they cast lots.
But you, O YHWH, do not be far away;
    my help, make haste to my aid.
Deliver my soul from the sword,
    my only [life] from the power of the dog.
Save me from the mouth of the lion!
    From[17] the horns of wild oxen you have answered me.[18]
Let me tell of your name to my brothers;
    in the midst of the congregation let me praise you.
Praise him, those who fear YHWH!
    Honor him, all the offspring of Jacob!
        Stand in awe of him, all the offspring of Israel!
For he has not despised nor detested the plight of the
        afflicted;
    and he has not hidden his face from me,[19]
        but hears when I cry to him for help.
From you comes my praise within the great congregation;
    my vows I will fulfill before those who fear him.
May the afflicted eat and be satisfied;
    may those who seek him praise YHWH;
        may[20] your hearts live forever.
All the ends of the earth will remember and turn to YHWH;
    and all the clans of the nations will bow down before
        you.
For dominion belongs to YHWH,
    and he rules over the nations.
Indeed,[21] to him all the powerful of the earth shall bow
        down;
    before him all who are about to descending to dust will
        kneel.
        My soul also lives for him.
Offspring shall serve him;
    it shall be told about my Lord to generations.
They shall come and tell of his righteousness
    to those yet to be born that he has done it.

No other psalm in the Psalter plumbs despair so deeply and at the same time scales the heights of praise so resolutely. Psalm 22 is unique because it stretches the genre of the complaint-petition as far as it can conceivably go—from both ends of the generic spectrum: complaint and praise.[22] Indeed, some have suggested that the psalm, given the prominence of its praise, is actually a hymn. But the psalm, in fact, defies either categorization. It extends radically in both directions from the middle, a middle that ironically leaves unaddressed the whiplash turn from complaint to praise, all within a single, short bicolon (v. 21).

What brings about such a sudden transition? One option is to posit, albeit hypothetically, an event that lies outside the psalmic text, such as an act of God that restores the speaker or, more modestly, a priestly intervention that offers assuring words from God, such as one finds in 12:5. The latter theory has been the dominant explanation in psalms studies.[23] But there are other possibilities. Instead of positing an intervening element at the moment of the psalmic shift to praise, another approach is to view the psalm as a whole from the psalm's endpoint, namely, from the vantage point of praise.[24] Thus, the complaint and its shift to praise are retrospective. The past is remembered so vividly that the speaker relives it in the present. Consequently, those few psalms that, for whatever reason, refuse to move toward praise (e.g., 39, 44, 88, and 89) remain squarely in the throes of complaint and/or petition. Their complaint, it must be noted, is not a thing of the past.

This retrospective approach, however, can rob the complaint of its seeming rhetorical immediacy. Are the complaints in these psalms simply a matter of recollection? To return to Psalm 13, the affirmation of trust and the vow to praise appear only in the final verse; the rest of the psalm is filled with complaint and petition. This psalm, as well as many others, is clearly weighted more toward complaint and petition than toward praise.

An opposing viewpoint asks: are the concluding expressions of praise in a given psalm meant to be uttered *in the midst of complaint*? Does the speaker anticipate future deliverance and, therefore, use praise to serve the speaker's aim to motivate God to action? Perhaps in some cases, as in Psalm 13, but not so, it seems, in Psalm 22. Any attempt to explain the surprising shift in these psalms must be done on a case-by-case basis, giving both defining generic elements—complaint and praise—their due, whether intrapsychically, rhetorically, theologically, or liturgically.[25]

What is clear is that the vast majority of the complaint-petition psalms conclude with praise. But is it praise that recalls a salvific act, or is it praise that anticipates the speaker's restoration? The "either-or" nature of such questions presumes a sort of once-and-for-all, "real time" realization that the Psalms themselves, written as they were for wide usage, may not have intended. In any case, the genre itself testifies to the coexistence of complaint and praise, of petition and joy. They are bound together, but not necessarily in any "right" sequential order. Certain psalms, in fact, reverse the movement from complaint to praise, as in the case of Psalm 89, whereby hymnic praise serves as a prelude to complaint and as a motivation for petition, as is more typical in the case of Mesopotamian prayers.[26] The interrelationship between complaint and praise in the biblical psalms remains something of a mystery, in part because it is manifested in different ways in different psalms.

Hymns or Praise Psalms

As the complaint-petition psalms typically conclude with an expression of praise, whether muted or pronounced, the praise psalms begin and end on the same resounding note. There are at least twenty-eight *bona fide* hymns in the Psalter. The shortest, Psalm 117, features two common elements that characterize the hymn.

> Praise YHWH, all you nations!
>> Acclaim him, all you peoples!
> For his benevolence has prevailed in our behalf,
>> and YHWH's faithfulness lasts forever.
> Hallelujah! (117:1-2)

The psalm opens with a command to give praise, a call to worship that includes not just Israel but all the nations. The second verse proclaims the reasons or basis for praise, drawn from God's character and activity. This mini-hymn concludes with the command "Hallelujah," itself a mini-call to praise ("Praise YH").

Hymns are distinguished from other psalmic genres by their calls or invitations to worship, which frequently bracket the reasons for such praise. In certain hymns, the call to praise dominates, such as in Psalm 148, which calls upon everything in creation to render praise to the creator, from top to bottom. In other hymns, the element of proclamation is dominant (e.g., 46, 48, 84, 87, 145). Proclamation in the praise psalms is delivered in a variety of ways. It can be cast in the third person, as with most psalms of praise, or in second-person address to God (8 and 104, for example). The elucidated basis for praise, moreover, focuses either on what God by nature is or does most generally (117), or on what God has done specifically in the past, in Israel's storied history, such as in the exodus and the settlement of the land (114, 135). One scholar has designated the former as "descriptive praise" and the latter as "narrative" or "declarative praise."[27] (The latter category, however, has more affinity with the so-called thanksgiving psalm, to be described in the next section.)

Some praise psalms, however, mix it up, such as Psalm 136.

> O give thanks to YHWH, for he is good,
>> for his benevolence is everlasting.
> O give thanks to the God of gods,
>> for his benevolence is everlasting.
> O give thanks to the Lord of lords,
>> for his benevolence is everlasting.
> To the one who alone does great wonders,
>> for his benevolence is everlasting.
> To the one who by understanding created the heavens,
>> for his benevolence is everlasting.
> To the one who spreads out the earth upon the waters,
>> for his benevolence is everlasting.
> To the one who fashioned the great lights,
>> for his benevolence is everlasting.
> The sun for dominion over the day,
>> for his benevolence is everlasting.
> The moon and stars for dominion over the night,
>> for his benevolence is everlasting.
> To the one who struck Egypt by their firstborn,
>> for his benevolence is everlasting,
> And who brought Israel out from among them,
>> for his benevolence is everlasting.
> With his strong arm and outstretched arm,
>> for his benevolence is everlasting.
> To the one who split the Red Sea in two,
>> for his benevolence is everlasting.
> And brought Israel through the midst of it,

for his benevolence is everlasting.
But swept off Pharaoh and his army into the Red Sea,
    for his benevolence is everlasting.

. . . .

[To the one] who remembered us in our low estate,
    for his benevolence is everlasting,
and has snatched us from our foes,
    for his benevolence is everlasting,
who provides food for all flesh,
    for his benevolence is everlasting.
O give thanks to the God of the heavens! (vv. 1-15, 23-26)

While the psalm begins and ends "descriptively," with reference to God's nature and ongoing work in creation (vv. 1-4, 25), the body of the psalm narrates God's past work in creating the world and in redeeming a people (vv. 5-24). Moreover, the second line of every verse repeats what the psalmist identifies as God's essential quality, "benevolence" (*hesed*), the fundamental basis of all God's actions—past, present, and future. Both descriptive and declarative is this resounding antiphonal psalm.

Thanksgiving Psalms

Intimately related to the hymn and to the complaint-petition psalm is the individual thanksgiving psalm. Compared to the complaint-petitions, thanksgiving psalms offer a complementary vantage point. In place of desperate pleas for help, the thanksgiving psalms provide concrete testimony to answered prayer and display unwavering confidence in God's care and power to deliver. But as in the complaints, human fragility and suffering are vividly acknowledged: "Out of my distress I called upon YHWH" (118:5a). But added in the same breath is an account of deliverance: "YHWH answered me and set me in a wide open place" (v. 5b). Briefer yet: "On the day I called, you answered me" (138:3; cf. Jonah 2:2).

On the one hand, the thanksgiving psalm can be seen as an extension or complement of the complaint-petition. Recalling a past crisis, thanksgiving psalms testify to answered petition. Central is the testimony: "I sought YHWH, and he answered me, and delivered me from all my fears" (34:4), which becomes generalized in verse 17: "When the righteous cry for help, YHWH hears, and rescues them from all their troubles." The testimony of God's responsive presence, as evidenced in the speaker's restored state, is characteristic of the thanksgiving psalms.

On the other hand, the language of thanksgiving is typically filled with expressions of praise, such as in the opening verse of Psalm 111. Indeed, the hymn and the thanksgiving psalm are sometimes difficult to distinguish, owing to common vocabulary. There is, moreover, a fine line between the proclamation of praise and the testimony of thanksgiving. The thanksgiving psalm revels in the rhetoric of personal testimony to what God has done for the individual or community in response to petition.[28] Psalm 107 constitutes perhaps the most elaborate thanksgiving psalm in the Psalter. It depicts four distinct situations of distress: lost in the wilderness, imprisonment, guilt and disease, and danger at sea. In each scenario, distress is depicted, petition is recalled, and God's salvific response is recounted, concluding with an exhortation to give thanks and praise.

The Generic Continuum

The complaint-petition, thanksgiving, and praise psalms constitute the three most common genres of the Psalter. The boundaries among them, however, can be "fuzzy." The psalms do not live by genre alone. The distinctions drawn from form-critical classifications are, in some cases, distinctions crossed by particular psalms. But genre study does help highlight how interrelated these main types are. Perhaps it is best to see these genre distinctions as part of a broad spectrum or continuum.

Complaint  Praise

Within that continuum, one finds the thanksgiving psalm situated squarely in the middle, inextricably tied to both: it recollects a time of complaint *and* renders praise to God in response to fulfilled petition. Even more remarkable is that the typical complaint-petition psalm contains elements that span the spectrum, with Psalm 22 being the most elaborate example. The complaint-petition constitutes the "backbone" of the Psalter not only because of its proliferation in the Psalter but also because of its structural breadth.

Other Types

The three main types discussed above by no means exhaust the generic variety of psalms. Other types pop up here and there throughout the Psalter. Related to the thanksgiving psalm is the "song of trust," whose most famous example is Psalm 23. The psalm conjoins two evocative metaphors for God, namely, shepherd and host. The psalm expresses a tone of confident trust in the God who protects the speaker and provides a well-filled "cup" (v. 5). In a similar psalm, the speaker professes a sense of abiding security in God, his or her "chosen portion" and "cup" (16:4).

Other types of psalms are less amenable to form-critical analysis but, nevertheless, can be categorized under more thematic characteristics. These would include the historical psalms, which recount ancient Israel's extensive history, selectively recounted by the psalmist and cast as thanksgiving and self-critique (78, 105–106, 135–136). Psalm 78, for example, tells of God's redemptive acts and the people's rebellious response, provoking God's anger. History is recounted not only as the history of Israel's salvation (*Heilsgeschichte*) across generations but also as the history of Israel's faults and God's punishment, its *Unheilsgeschichte*.

Also well attested are the so-called royal psalms (2, 18, 20–21, 45, 72, 101, 110, 118, 144:1-11). They exhibit no fixed literary pattern but all deal, in some form or fashion, with the earthly king. Psalm 2, for example, celebrates the king as God's anointed, indeed God's "son," within the boiling cauldron of international conflict. Psalm 110 appears to be part of a coronation ceremony, while Psalm 45 contains the liturgy of a king's wedding. Psalm 72 outlines the solemn duties of the king, including care for the "poor" and "needy."

Related to the royal psalms are the enthronement psalms (24, 29, 47, 93, 95–99). But instead of celebrating the rule of the earthly king, these psalms acclaim God's kingship, sometimes accompanied with the enthronement cry, "YHWH reigns!" (93:1; 96:10; 97:1; 99:1). It is easy to imagine such psalms being used at major festivals to commemorate God's victory over chaos and sovereign reign over the cosmos.

Not unrelated, also, are the "songs of Zion" (46, 48, 76, 84, 87, 121–122). According to Psalm 2, a royal psalm, God's anointed is established "on Zion, my holy hill" (v. 6). In the Zion psalms, Zion is celebrated as the habitat for divinity, the place of God's holy abode, protected from raging enemies. Psalm 48 gives the reader a virtual tour of impenetrable Zion.

> Great is YHWH, and highly praised
>> in the city of our God.
> His holy mountain, beautiful in elevation, is the joy of all the
>>> earth;
>> Mount Zion, in the far north, is the city of the great king.
> By its citadels,
>> God proves himself to be a stronghold.
> For, indeed, the kings assembled themselves,
>> advancing together.
> When they saw it, they were struck dumb;
>> they became terrified and fled in alarm.
> Trembling seized them there,
>> like a woman in labor pains.
> Or when an easterly wind smashes
>> the ships of Tarshish.
> As we have heard, so have we seen,
>> in the city of YHWH of hosts, in the city of our God.
>>> It is God who establishes it forever. *Selah*
> We ponder your benevolence, O God,
>> in the midst of your temple.
> As is your name, O God, so also is your praise
>> [extending] to the ends of the earth.
>>> Your right hand is filled with victory.
> Let Mount Zion be glad;
>> let the daughters [towns] of Judah rejoice,
>>> on account of your judgments.
> Walk around Zion; encircle it;
>> count its towers.
> Scrutinize its ramparts; inspect its citadels,
>> that you may declare to the next generation:
> "This is God, our God forever and ever!"
>> It is he who will lead us.

So enamored with Zion's formidable presence, the speaker equates Zion, metaphorically, with God. The mere sight of Zion inspires fear among foreign kings and pride and joy among the city's citizens. Zion is the sign and seal of God's holy power, to be passed on to each and every generation. According to the psalm, God has an edifice complex.

Two other categories of psalms are closely aligned, the *tôrâ* and didactic (or so-called wisdom) psalms. The former psalms refer specifically to God's *tôrâ* or "teaching," namely, Psalms 1, 19, and 119. The last psalm, the so-called "Psalm of the Law," is the lengthiest psalm of the Psalter (176 verses), with its entire content singularly devoted to the efficacy and value of divinely imparted instruction. The didactic psalms, an admittedly loose category, share the rhetorical aim of giving instruction about life before God rather than eliciting praise or prayer. Diverse though they are, such psalms include at least 32, 34, 37, 49, 73, and (111) 112. All either adopt a didactic or admonitory tone (32:9; 34:12-15; 37:8; 49:17) or provide a profile of virtuous conduct or appropriated wisdom (73, 112).

Some psalms, of course, do not fit neatly into any category described above, or they fit into more than one (see 50, 68, 82, 108, 126, 129). Nevertheless, knowing the genres can aid in following the structural logic and movement of many, if not most, psalms. Genres provide flexible templates by which to appreciate what is both common and distinctive of every psalm.

Psalms without Generic Restrictions

As Gunkel argued, identifying the genre of a psalm offers a clue about how the psalm may have been used or intended for use. The temptation, however, is to assume that every psalm was functionally restricted to its generically reflected setting. Psalm 30 provides a telling example.

> I extol you, YHWH, for you have drawn me up,
>> and you have not let my enemies rejoice over me.
> YHWH, my God, I cried out to you,
>> and you healed me.
> YHWH, you brought me up from Sheol;
>> you revived me from among those descending to the pit.
> Sing praises to YHWH, O faithful ones;
>> give thanks to his holy renown.
> For (only) a moment is his anger, but a lifetime is his favor;
>> while weeping tarries in the night, rejoicing is set for the
>>> morning.
> Yet I once said in my ease,
>> "I am forever unshakable."

YHWH, by your favor you affixed (me) as a mighty
    mountain;
  (but when) you hid your face, I was devastated.
So to you, YHWH, I called;
  to the Lord I made petition:
"What savage gain is there in my blood,
  in my descending into the pit?
Does the dust offer you thanks?
  Does it proclaim your faithfulness?
Hear, YHWH, and grant me mercy;
  YHWH, be my helper."
You have turned my wailing into dancing for me;
  you have removed my sackcloth,
    and girded me with joy,
so that (my) inner being[29] will sing praises to you
  and not keep silent;
  YHWH, my God, I will give you thanks forever.

By content and form, Psalm 30 is a *bona fide* thanksgiving psalm. It opens on a personal note of praise and recounts a time of distress in which God intervened and delivered the speaker (vv. 2-4), leading him or her to call others to praise and declare God's kindness (vv. 5-6). The liturgical gears, however, shift abruptly in the second half of the psalm. Verse 7 either introduces testimony of another time of distress or offers a different perspective on the same past distress. In any case, this second scenario features a petition and a complaint (vv. 9-11), followed by a testimony of the speaker's reversal of fortune whereby joy takes the place of mourning (v. 12), prompting another expression of praise and thanksgiving, which concludes the psalm (v. 13).

One can imagine that this thanksgiving psalm, as with all individual thanksgiving psalms, was composed for and used by individuals who experienced God's healing power (v. 3b) and deliverance from enemies (v. 2b), even from death (v. 4). The call to praise in verse 5, however, suggests that such testimony was given publicly in the setting of worship. But that is not the end of the matter. The complication in this generic reconstruction is that the superscription (which I conveniently omitted in the translation above) suggests another setting:

A Psalm <A Dedicatory Song for the Temple> of David.

According to its title, this allegedly individual thanksgiving psalm was actually used to dedicate the temple, a function that cannot at all be inferred from the psalm's content and form. For reasons unknown, this psalm functioned liturgically at a temple dedication, perhaps at the Feast of Dedication (Hanukkah) celebrating the cleansing of the temple by Judas Maccabeus in 164 B.C.E. In view of its title, the psalm's setting as a thanksgiving psalm is reconfigured in a way that transforms the testimony of an individual's passage from distress to wholeness into a testimony shared by many in the temple. With the temple as its setting (as stated by the superscription), the speaking subject becomes the temple community. Could it be that an anonymous individual's travail profiled in the psalm comes to represent the temple's own suffering, its destruction and desecration? In any case, the psalm melds together the individual, community, and temple as testimony of past distress turns toward peals of praise for the temple's restoration.

This one example shows all too clearly that the Psalms were not restricted to their generic settings. Given the stark difference between a reconstructed setting of a psalm, as informed by its genre, and its actual usage, as indicated in the superscription, many psalms were evidently used and reused in varying ways. Call it psalmic recycling. In fact, certain psalms in the Psalter reflect just that. Psalms 14 and 53, for example, appear identical at first glance, but a closer inspection reveals important differences (see especially 14:5-6 and 53:5), including the superscriptions. Psalm 108, moreover, seems to have borrowed parts of Psalms 57 and 60 (see 57:7-11; 60:5-12; 108:1-5, 6-13). For ancient Israel, the Psalms evidently held no copyright restrictions. They could be performed in a variety of ways. Their performative versatility is the topic of the next chapter.

CHAPTER 4

PSALMS AS PERFORMANCE

The Psalter bursts with activity: shouting, singing, scream-
ing, crying, walking, trembling, dancing, bowing, praying,
and lifting are all captured in the Psalms. Conveying an
urgent sense of immediacy, the Psalms compel readers to take
part, indeed get caught up, in the intensely physical activities of
praise and proclamation, of complaint and petition. As an
"emphatic, balanced, and elevated kind of discourse," psalmic
poetry is, according to Robert Alter, "perhaps ultimately rooted in
a magical conception of language as potent performance."[1]
Magical or not, psalmic language is clearly performative, and its
performative power lies not so much in the eye of the beholder as
in the mouth of the reader. Through recitation, the psalmist's
words become the reader's words, whether performed individually or corporately. The reader of psalms is compelled to take up
the subject position of the speaker—"I" or "we"—and is carried
forward by the psalm's rhetorical movement. Reading the Psalms
is much like riding a rollercoaster, ascending the heights of praise
and plumbing the depths of lament, twisting and turning, all
within only a few verses. Warning: Reading the Psalms can induce

61

queasiness or cause whiplash! The reader of psalms, wittingly or unwittingly, does much more than read. That "much more" is the focus of this chapter.

The range of the Psalter's "performance" is stunning, covering everything from mourning to dancing, from the verbal to the kinesthetic. Even the emotionally laden language of the Psalms can indicate performative activity. As Gary Anderson notes, the expressions of joy and mourning within a cultic context are not simply outpourings of emotion; they are behavioral, ritually based activities.[2] This chapter samples the performative dimensions of certain psalms, beginning with the verbal and concluding with specific activities prescribed in the poetry, particularly as they relate to worship and instruction.

Verbal

The Psalms are rife with references to verbal activity. If complaint-petitions, hymns, and songs of thanksgiving constitute the generic foundations of psalmic poetry, then beseeching, praising, and proclaiming are the fundamental activities of the speaking subject. If the Psalter were a temple, no "sanctuary of silence" would it be.[3] Rare it is that the reader is exhorted to be still and silent before God.[4] More often than not, the psalmic speaker is engaged in broadcasting his or her distress to God and others.

> With my voice I cry out to YHWH;
>   with my voice I plead to YHWH.
> I pour out my complaint before him;
>   I declare my distress before him. (142:1-2)

The speaker is no sanctuary wallflower. In corporate worship, the very rafters seem to shake "with joyous cries and songs of thanksgiving, a multitude making festival" (42:4).

In the psalms of the individual, the speaker is most engaged in a verbal exchange with God, whether in complaint or in praise: "I cry aloud to YHWH, and he answers me from his holy mountain" (3:4). Or in the throes of desperate prayer: "Answer me when I call, O God of my vindication!" (4:2).

> My God, my God, why have you forsaken me?
>   (Why) so far from my cry, the words of my screaming?

My God, I cry out by day, but you do not answer;
  at night I have no relief. (22:1-2)

Impassioned, compelling communication is not the only measure of discourse in the Psalms. Certain psalms acknowledge the speaker's inarticulate expressions of pain and distress:

Utterly numbed and crushed am I,
  I shriek from the groaning of my heart.
O Lord, all my longing is before you;
  my sighing is not hidden from you. (38:8-9)

I think of God and I groan;
  I ponder as my spirit grows faint. *Selah*
You have held my eyelids open;
  so discombobulated am I that I cannot speak. (77:3-4)

Sighing, groaning, shrieking: such are the expressions of pain that cannot be captured into words. And then there is the silencing power of pain.

When I kept silent, my bones wore out,
  so also as I screamed all day long.
For day and night your hand was heavy upon me;
  my sap[5] dried up[6] as by the dry heat of summer. *Selah*
So I acknowledged my sin to you,
  and my guilt I did not cover up.
I said, "I confess my transgressions to YHWH,"
  and you lifted off the guilt of my sin. *Selah* (32:3-5)

In this thanksgiving psalm, silence and inarticulate screams are poetically correlated. The remedy in the psalm is speech, specifically confessional speech, which results in a liberating release from God's hand and the speaker's guilt. Direct discourse in verse 5 stresses the redemptive agency of spoken confession.

Another passage that charts the movement from silence to speech is found in the opening verses of Psalm 39.

I said, "I will guard my ways from sinning with my tongue;
  I will keep a muzzle on my mouth
    so long as the wicked are before me."
So I was mute, silent; I hushed myself, but to no avail;
  my pain flared up.

My heart grew hot within me;
    in my pondering a fire burned.
        I spoke with my tongue:
"Reveal to me, YHWH, my end!
    What is the measure of my days?
        Let me know how brief a time I have left." (39:1-4)

As in Psalm 32, silence is correlated with unalleviated pain. Acknowledging that speech has been a source of sin, the supplicant declares his or her intent to remain silent, but to no avail. Pain burns within the speaker, and the only recourse is to break the silence and address God directly, demanding disclosure of the supplicant's fate. A comparable statement regarding the speaker's silence occurs later:

I became mute; I did not open my mouth,
    for you have made it so.
Remove your stroke from me!
    I am utterly spent from the blow(s) of your hand.
        With reproofs you chasten a person for iniquity,
and like a moth you dissolve away one's desirable things.
        Indeed, all humanity is mere breath. *Selah*
Hear my prayer, YHWH!
    Listen to my cry!
Do not be deaf to my tears,
    for I am with you as a sojourner,
        an alien like all my ancestors. (39:9-13)

As in verse 3, the speaker recalls his or her vow of silence, but all the while speaking in urgent petition! The speaker blames God for imposing silence. But once silenced, the "I" now speaks, and with a vengeance: words of petition burst forth from the supplicant's mouth. The formulation of speech marks the starting point of resolution and restoration. As the speaker breaks the silence, so God is urged to do the same and, thereby, act upon the speaker's petition.

    As a whole, the climax of psalmic discourse is reached in the expression of praise and proclamation.

I will give thanks, YHWH, with all my heart;
    I will tell of all your wondrous deeds.

I will rejoice and exult in you;
 I will sing praises to your name, *Elyon*. (9:2-3)

The act of singing praise and giving thanks, as many psalms prescribe, is to be accompanied by music:

Give thanks to YHWH with the lyre!
 Perform praise to him with the ten-stringed harp!
Sing to him a new song;
 play skillfully with a blast of joy. (33:2-3)

Let me come to the altar of God, to God,
 the joy of my rejoicing,
so that I will give you thanks with the lyre,
 O God, my God. (43:4)

God has come up with a shout,
 YHWH with the sound of the *shofar*.
Make music to God, make music!
 Make music to our king, make music!
For God is king of all the earth.
 Make music with a *maśkîl*! (47:5-7)

I will also give you thanks with the harp,
 for your faithfulness, my God.
  I will perform for you with the lyre,
 O Holy One of Israel.
My lips will rejoice aloud when I perform for you,
 my soul, also, which you have redeemed. (71:22-23)

Rejoice aloud to God, our strength;
 shout for joy to the God of Jacob.
Raise a song and strike the hand drum,[7]
 the sweet lyre with the harp.
Blow the *shofar* at the new moon,
 at the full moon, for our feast day. (81:2-4)

I shall sing a new song to you, O God;
 Upon the ten-stringed harp I shall perform for you.
             (144:9)

Not coincidentally, the final psalm provides the most exhaustive list of musical instruments in the Psalter:

> Hallelujah!
> Praise God in his sanctuary!
>   Praise him in his mighty firmament!
> Praise him for his mighty acts!
>   Praise him as befits his surpassing greatness!
> Praise him with *shofar* blast![8]
>   Praise him with lute and lyre!
> Praise him with drum and dance!
>   Praise him with strings and pipe![9]
> Praise him with resounding cymbals!
>   Praise him with clashing cymbals!
> Let everything that has breath praise YHWH!
> Hallelujah! (150:1-6)

In a mere six verses, winds, strings, and percussion are all enlisted in an orchestral production of song and dance, a vibrant cacophony of praise to "God in his sanctuary...in his mighty firmament." Singing God's praises was no solo act (e.g., 149:3).

The Psalms not only declare the speaker's praise but also command it. After proclaiming his deliverance from Sheol, the speaker in Psalm 30 enjoins:

> Sing praises to YHWH, O faithful ones;
>   give thanks to his holy renown.[10] (30:4)

Psalm 34 takes on a more invitational tone:

> I shall bless YHWH at all times;
>   always in my mouth is his praise.
> In YHWH do I boast;
>   may the lowly hear and rejoice.
> Magnify YHWH with me,
>   and let us exalt his name together. (34:1-3)

Such praise and proclamation come not simply from the mouth (and "tongue") but also from the speaker's "bones" (35:10; 51:8), "soul" (35:9), "heart" (13:5; 28:7), and even "liver."[11]

As praise infuses itself deep within a person's marrow, filling his or her whole body, it also expands, like ripples in a pond, far beyond the individual and the worshiping community. The circle of praise encompasses all peoples (67:5) and all the earth, nature included (66:1, 4; 69:34), indeed both heaven and earth (148)![12] In short, the Psalms have all to do with verbal communication, whether to God in praise, prayer, and confession or to others in proclamation and instruction. The Psalms serve to wrest powerful speech out of stultifying silence and from unlikely places and agencies.

Kinesthetic

In addition to active speech, the Psalms also refer to certain kinds of activities that involve bodily movement, either parts of the body or the body in its entirety. In any case, the Psalms provide a kinesis of prayer and praise.

Hands-on Activity

A number of psalmic texts either prescribe or describe the raising of hands, particularly in association with God's presence.

> Hear the voice of my pleading as I cry out to you,
>> when *I lift up my hands* to your holy inner sanctum.
>>> (28:2)

> Now bless YHWH, all you servants of YHWH,
>> who stand by night in YHWH's house!
> *Lift up your hands* to the holy place,
>> and bless YHWH.
> May YHWH, maker of heaven and earth,
>> bless you from Zion. (134:1-3)

> Because your benevolence is better than life;
>> my lips praise you.
> So I bless you as long as I live;
>> in your name *I lift up my hands*. (63:4-5)

> May my prayer be set before you as incense,
>> *my upraised hands* as an evening offering. (141:2)

The lifting of the hands designates a posture of petition as well as of praise. In the final example, hand-lifting signifies offering, specifically incense offering (cf. Exod 30:7-8; Ps 116:13).

Certain psalms also enjoin the clapping of hands, accompanied by verbal praise, whether by the worshiping community or by the community of creation:

> *Clap hands,* all you peoples;
>> shout to God with joyous cry.
> For YHWH *Elyon* is fearsome,
>> great king over all the earth. (47:1-2)

> With trumpets and the *shofar* blast,
>> shout for joy before YHWH the King!
> Let the sea and its fullness roar,
>> the world and its inhabitants.
> Let the torrents *clap their hands,*
>> and the mountains together rejoice aloud,
> before YHWH, for he is coming to judge the earth;
>> he will judge the world rightly and the peoples fairly.
>>> (98:6-9)

In both examples, clapping signifies not only praise but fear, whose object is the king and judge of all creation.

Whole Body Activity

Other kinesthetic activities in worship involve movement of the whole body, including dancing:

> Sing to YHWH a new song,
>> his praise in the assembly of the faithful.
> Let Israel be glad in its Maker;
>> let the children of Zion rejoice in their king.
> Let them praise his name in dance;
>> with drum and lyre let them perform for him.
>>> (149:1-3 [see also 150:4; 30:11])

In dance, praise gets its choreography. Dancing is also included in the list of musical instruments to be performed in worship in 150:4. (For a particularly revealing scene of worship that includes dancing, see the account of the ark of the covenant's procession into Jerusalem in 2 Samuel 6).

Also part of kinesthetic praise is the practice of bowing down before God's presence or toward the temple.

By your abundant benevolence, I will enter your house;
  I will *bow down* in awe of you in your holy temple. (5:7)

Exalt YHWH, our God!
  Bow down at his footstool!
    Holy is he! (99:5)

I give you thanks with my whole heart;
  before the gods I perform for you.
I *bow down* toward your holy temple,
  and I give thanks to your name for your benevolence and
    faithfulness,
for you have made your name great,
  your word above everything.[13] (138:1-2)

Affirming the unmatched sovereignty of God (see 22:29), the posture of self-prostration is not limited to the worshiping community, but includes "all the nations":

There is none like you among the gods, O Lord,
  nor anything like your works.
All the nations that you made will come,
  and *bow down* before you, O Lord,
    and give glory to your name.
For you are great and a worker of wonders;
  you are God, you alone. (86:8-10)

The bowed or prostrate posture serves to acknowledge the superior, indeed superlative, presence of God. In these cited psalms, "bow down" is set parallel with entering God's presence. Movement, thus, is crucial in the Psalter. Entering the place of God's presence, among other things, involves ascent.

Who shall ascend YHWH's hill?
  Who shall stand in his holy place? (24:3)

Let us come before his face with thanksgiving!
  With songs of joy let us raise a joyful shout to him! (95:2)

Enter his gates with thanksgiving, his courts with praise!
  Give thanks to him; bless his name! (100:4)

Open for me the gates of righteousness,
that I may enter through them and give thanks to YH.
This is the gate of YHWH;
(only) the righteous shall enter through it. (118:19-20)

"Ascend," "come," "enter": movement is required in the topography of worship, which finds its locus on top of God's holy hill, in the temple of Zion. A more formal designation of such movement is found in Psalms 68 and 122.

Your procession, O God, they saw,
the procession of my God, my king, into the sanctuary.
First come the singers, then the instrumentalists,
and between them the young women playing hand
drums.
Bless God in the great congregation,
YHWH, from Israel's fountain.
There is Benjamin, though little, leading them,
the princes of Judah, their speaker,[14]
princes of Zebulun, the princes of Naphtali. (68:24-28)

I rejoiced with those who said to me,
"Let us go to YHWH's house."
Our feet are standing,
within your gates, O Jerusalem.
Jerusalem is built as a city
joined together in unity.
There the tribes go up, the tribes of YH.
Such is the decree for Israel—
to give thanks to YHWH's name. (122:1-4)

Psalm 68 offers an elaborate description of a temple procession that involves numerous singers and musicians of various instruments, followed by representatives of various tribes. Psalm 122 moves from the individual to the corporate experience of entering into temple worship. Once in the temple, the altar becomes the prominent focus of attention, as indicated in the following psalms.

Send forth your light and your truth; they shall guide me.
May they bring me to your holy mountain,
to your dwelling place.

Let me come to God's altar, to God, the joy of my rejoicing,
  that I may give you thanks with the lyre, O God, my God.
                                                    (43:3-4)

I wash my hands in innocence,
  and encircle your altar, YHWH,
to proclaim aloud thanksgiving,
  to recount all your wondrous deeds.
YHWH, I adore the beauty[15] of your abode,
  the dwelling place of your glory. (26:6-8)

In these two psalms, the destination point in the temple is the
altar, to which one approaches and encircles (see also 118:27). It
is the altar of sacrifice (51:19).

Sacrifice

In addition to being a house of prayer and praise, the temple is
also marked in the Psalms as the site of offering and sacrifice
(51:19). Several references are made in the Psalter to sacrificial
offerings, but not all of those references hold the same perspective.

Do good to Zion by your favor;
  rebuild the walls of Jerusalem.
Then you shall take pleasure in right sacrifices—
  burnt offerings and whole offerings—
    then bulls will be sacrificed on your altar.
                                       (51:18-19)

I come into your house with burnt offerings;
  I will fulfill my vows to you,
    which my lips have uttered,
  and my mouth has spoken in my distress.
Burnt offerings of fatlings I will offer to you,
  with the smoke of sacrificed rams;
    I will make an offering of bulls and goats. *Selah* (66:13-15)

Give to YHWH, O clans of the peoples!
  Give to YHWH glory and power!
Give to YHWH the glory of his name!
  Offer gifts and enter his courts! (96:7-8)

71

In these examples, various forms of sacrifice seem to be an indispensable part of worship. Other psalms, however, hold a different view of the necessity of sacrifice:

> Sacrifice and offering you do not delight in,
>> instead you have opened my ears.
>>> Burnt offering and guilt offering you do not require.
>>>> (40:6)

> For you do not desire sacrifice;
>> were I to offer burnt offering,[16] you would not accept it.
> My sacrifice, O God,[17] is a broken spirit;
>> a broken and crushed heart, O God, you do not despise.
>>> (51:16-17)

The following psalm, cast as divine discourse, provides a rationale for God's rejection of sacrifices in the previously cited text.

> "Hear, O my people, and I shall speak, O Israel;
>> I shall testify against you. I am God, your God.
> I reprove you not for your sacrifices;
>> your burnt offerings are ever before me.
> I shall accept no bulls from your house,
>> or goats from your folds.
> For every wild animal of the forest is mine,
>> cattle on a thousand hills.
> I know every bird of the mountains;
>> even the bugs[18] of the fields are mine.
> If I were hungry, I would not tell you,
>> for the world and all that fills it are mine.
> Do I eat the meat of bulls,
>> or drink the blood of goats?
> Present to God a sacrifice of thanksgiving,
>> and pay to *Elyon* your vows.
> Call upon me on the day of distress;
>> I will deliver you so that you shall glorify me." (50:7-15)

This extended admonition makes clear that God does not hunger for, much less consume, flesh and blood, for all creation belongs to God. The creator of all claims all, owns all. Nevertheless, God expects sacrifice of a different sort. The object of divine desire is "a sacrifice of thanksgiving," whatever that may entail,[19] and the payment of vows (v. 14). Other psalms also stress the import of such an offering:

> In God I trust; I am not afraid.
>> What can any person do to me?
> My vows to you, O God, oblige me;
>> I will pay thanksgiving offerings to you.
> For you have saved my life from death,
>> indeed, my feet from stumbling,
>>> so that I may walk before God in the light of life.
>>>> (56:11-13)

> To you I offer a sacrifice of thanksgiving,
>> and call on YHWH's name.
> My vows I shall pay to YHWH,
>> in the very presence of all the people,
> in the courts of YHWH's house,
>> in your midst, O Jerusalem. (116:17-19)

In Psalms 50, 56, and 116, cited above, the offering of thanksgiving is coupled with the payment of vows, another essential activity of worship, according to the Psalter:

> From you comes my praise within the great congregation;
>> my vows I shall fulfill before those who fear him. (22:25)

> So shall I forever sing praises to your name,
>> as I fulfill my vows day after day. (61:8)

> To you silence is praise, O God in Zion,
>> and to you a vow is fulfilled. (65:1)

> I come into your house with burnt offerings;
>> I shall fulfill my vows to you. (66:13)

> What shall I give back to YHWH,
>> for all his benefits to me?
> I will lift up the cup of salvation;
>> I will call on YHWH's name.
> My vows I shall repay to YHWH;
>> in the very presence of all his people.
. . . .

To you I offer a sacrifice of thanksgiving,
    and call on YHWH's name.
My vows I will pay to YHWH,
    in the very presence of all the people,
in the courts of YHWH's house,
    in your midst, O Jerusalem. (116:12-14, 17-19)

Make vows to YHWH your God and fulfill them;
    let all around him bear gifts to the fearsome one. (76:11)

In these examples, the payment of vows is associated with burnt offering, thanksgiving, praise, and giving tribute.

Dwelling

Though not as specific an activity as the ones discussed above, dwelling in the place of worship, the temple, is frequently mentioned in the Psalms.

As one who dwells in the shelter of *Elyon*,
    who abides in the shadow of *Shaddai*,
I say to YHWH, "My refuge and my stronghold,
    my God in whom I trust." (91:1-2)

Most famous, perhaps, is the final line of Psalm 23:

Only goodness and kindness will pursue me
    all the days of my life,
so that may I dwell in the house of YHWH
    as long as I live. (23:6)

But the all-consuming longing to "dwell" in God's dwelling place is attested in several additional psalms, and for various reasons.

One thing I ask of YHWH, which I seek:
    To dwell in YHWH's house all the days of my life,
        to behold YHWH's beauty
            and gaze longingly on his temple.
For he hides me in his shelter on the day of evil;
    he conceals me with the covering of his tent;
        he sets me high on a rock. (27:4-5)

Hear, O God, my cry;
    attend to my prayer.

. . . .
Let me dwell[20] in your tent forever;
    let me take refuge in the shelter of your wings. (61:1, 4)

Even the sparrow has found a home, the swallow her nest,
    where she has laid her young beside your altars,
        YHWH of hosts, my king and my God.
How happy are those who dwell in your house,
    praising you continually. *Selah*
. . . .
For better is a day in your courts
    than a thousand elsewhere;
I would rather stand at the threshold
    of the house of my God,
        than dwell in the tents of wickedness. (84:3-4, 10)

As refuge, hiding place, tent, and rock, the temple is an object of fervent desire, a place for dwelling, indeed, a place to call home, even if it means "standing" only at its threshold. So strong is the longing for a place in God's "house" that even God calls it a "resting place" (132:14) and sparrows find their nesting place in it.

Psalm 27 adds two additional forms of activity that have their home in the temple: "gaze" and "inquire" (v. 4). The first refers to beholding the temple and God's presence therein, perhaps comparable to what Psalm 48 describes from the outside:

Let Mount Zion be glad;
    let the daughters [towns] of Judah rejoice,
        because of your judgments.
Walk around Zion; encircle it;
    count its towers.
Scrutinize its ramparts; inspect its citadels,
    so that you may declare to the next generation:
"This is God, our God forever and ever!"
    It is he who will lead us. (48:11-15)

Unfortunately, we do not have a comparable tour of the temple's interior. As for "inquiring" (*bqr*) within God's temple, Psalm 73 reports a telling incident:

Look, such are the wicked,
    always at ease, piling up wealth.

75

Surely in vain I have kept my heart pure,
    and washed my hands in innocence.
. . . .
And when I tried to understand these things,
    it was torment in my eyes,
until I entered God's sanctuary,
    and discerned (*byn*) their end. (73:12-13, 16-17)

The speaker is perplexed by the prosperity of the wicked. Resolution, however, is reached within the hallowed walls of the temple, where the speaker has "discerned" the fate of the wicked. Whether through a vision or through a dream, or simply by being awestruck by the temple's grandeur, the speaker becomes convinced that God's punishment of the wicked is imminent, that their fate is sealed (v. 27). But by whatever means, it is there in the sanctuary, in "nearness to God" (v. 28), that the speaker finds an answer. The temple is the locus of revelation.

Shaping Desire

As we have seen, the distinctly performative language of the Psalms takes readers into various activities: recitation, movement, singing, complaining, proclaiming, entering, dwelling, and, most broadly, worshiping. Undergirding all these activities, however, is a more fundamental operation at work: the shaping of desire. As a whole, the Psalms inculcate a desire for God and God's temple:

As a doe longs for ravines of water,
    so my soul longs for you, O God.
My soul thirsts for God, the living God.
    When shall I come and see God's face? (42:1-2)

O God, my God, for you I search.
    My soul thirsts for you;
my flesh grows faint for you
    in a dry and wearied land, with no water.
So I have looked for you in the sanctuary,
    to behold your power and glory. (63:1-2)

My soul longs, indeed it faints, for YHWH's courts;
    my heart and flesh cry aloud to the living God. (84:2)

I have become a stranger to my brothers,
    an alien to my mother's sons.
For zeal for your house has consumed me;
    the insults of those who insult you have fallen on me.
                                                    (69:8-9)

Whom else do I have in the heavens?
    Besides you there is nothing I desire on earth.
Though my flesh and my heart may fail,
    God is the rock of my heart and my portion forever.
                                                    (73:25-26)

"Zeal" in 69:9 is the same word for "jealousy" (*qin'āh*) elsewhere (cf. Exod 20:5; 34:14; Deut 4:24). Whether as consuming zeal or unquenchable thirst, the desire for God is inscribed as the highest and most intense yearning. In the psalmists' eyes, God is the ultimate object of desire. According to Psalms 63 and 84, the yearning for God and the longing for God's temple are inseparably bound together. Dwelling in God's presence, manifested in the temple, is the highest desideratum (e.g., 63:5; 84:11). "From Zion, the perfection of beauty, God shines forth," intones Ps 50:2. Or "His holy mountain, beautiful in elevation, is the joy of all the earth" (48:2-3).

It is no coincidence, then, that such ardent language also includes occasional references to "love":

I love you, YHWH, my strength. (18:2)

YHWH, I love the beauty of your abode,
    the dwelling place of your glory. (26:8)

May all who seek you rejoice and be glad in you,
    and may those who love your salvation always say,
        "God is Great!" (70:4)

Desire, however, is by no means one-sided. The psalmist's desire for God's abode is, at least in two psalms, matched by God's desire.

For YHWH has chosen Zion;
    he desired it for his residence.
"This is my resting place forevermore;
    here I shall reside, for I have desired it." (132:13-14)

O mountain of God, O mountain of Bashan;
    O many-peaked mountain, O mountain of Bashan!
Why do you gaze with envy, O many-peaked mountains,
    at the mountain that God desires for his dwelling,
        where YHWH himself dwells forever?
God's chariots are twice ten thousand,
    thousands ad infinitum,
The Lord among them, (the God of) Sinai,
    came into the sanctuary. (68:15-18)

In addition to God and God's abode, God's *tôrâ* is also the object of the speaker's love. The longest psalm of the Psalter, for example, is also the most passionate of psalms:

O how I love your *tôrâ*!
    All day long it is my deliberation! (119:97)

And I find delight in your commandments,
    which I love.
And I shall lift up my hands to your commandments,
    which I love,
        and deliberate on your statutes. (119:47-48)

Therefore, I love your commandments
    more than gold, even fine gold. (119:127)

I hate falsehood, indeed, I abhor it;
    it is your *tôrâ* that I love. (119:163)

In this near-mystical meditation, the speaker is lovesick over God's "law." As God's *tôrâ* receives the speaker's ardent love, it awakens, in turn, the speaker's desire for righteousness and understanding (vv. 40, 106, 144).

If cultivating desire for God is a fundamental aim of many psalms, then worship, in its various forms, is the corporate expression of such desire. How worship was actually performed with the Psalms in ancient Israel has been a focus of study and speculation for more than a century.

Worship

Form-criticism, beginning with Gunkel, has not only advanced the taxonomic impulse to categorize psalms in terms of shared features; it has also launched great interest in the performative settings of psalms in worship. From content alone, many psalms, some already discussed, clearly reflect the activity of worship: references are made throughout the Psalter to festal events (81:3), temple visits (5:7; 65:4; 122:1-2), processions (24:7-10; 42:4; 118:26-27), sacrifices (4:5; 51:19; 107:22; 116:17), benedictions (115:14-15; 121:3-8; 134:3), and payment of vows (22:26; 61:8; 65:2; 76:12). Some psalms reflect antiphonal singing (118 and 136), while others prescribe the accompaniment of various musical instruments in worship (149:3; 150:3-5). It is clear that many, if not most, psalms were crafted to be performed with music.

From the legal and historical narratives of the Hebrew Bible, we learn that ancient Israel led a rich liturgical life.[21] In addition to regular services held daily, on the sabbaths, and at the new moon,[22] Israel had three "appointed festivals" that required the participation of all Israelite males:[23] (1) Festival of Unleavened Bread and Passover, (2) Festival of Weeks (or Pentecost), and (3) Festival of Ingathering (or Festival of Tabernacles or Booths). All were associated with the agricultural seasons. The first festival was the Feast of Unleavened Bread (late March/early April), commemorating the new barley harvest. It later came to be conjoined with the Passover Festival, commemorating the release from bondage in Egypt (Exod 12; cf. Lev 23:4-8). The Festival of Weeks took place seven weeks after the beginning of the barley harvest, coinciding with the beginning of the wheat harvest. The third festival, Ingathering, was held in the fall after the harvest of fruits, olives, and grapes (late September/early October), just prior to the beginning of the rainy season. According to Leviticus 23, this fall festival complex consisted of three parts: (1) a festival "commemorated with trumpet blasts" and marked by "complete rest" (v. 24); (2) the Day of Atonement, marked by penitence (vv. 26-32); and (3) the Festival of Booths, commemorating the wilderness wanderings (vv. 33-43). Each event required the presentation of burnt offerings (vv. 25, 27, 37). In all three annual festivals, "the choicest of the first fruits of [the] ground" were dedicated to God in "the house of YHWH" (Exod 23:19). Deuteronomy 26:1-11 offers liturgical instruction on the presentation of the "first fruits," complete with a historical catechesis recounting Israel's release from Egyptian bondage and the settlement of the land.

Were some of the psalms composed and used for these festivals?

Absolutely. Thanksgiving for God's agricultural bounty (e.g., 65), praise for God's providential work on behalf of Israel (e.g., 136), confession of sin and penitence (e.g., 51)—all seem to have their places in such festivals. The Festival of Booths, mentioned in Zech 14:16-20, was apparently the defining occasion to "worship the King, YHWH of hosts" (v. 16). Perhaps not coincidentally, the enthronement psalms of the Psalter (47, 93, 95–99) provide the liturgical medium for worshiping the divine sovereign. The Septuagint version of Psalm 29, moreover, adds to the superscription "on the final day of the Tabernacle Festival."

Israel's liturgical life, however, was by no means confined to these three festivals and other regulated times of worship. When a new king assumed the throne, a coronation ceremony was held (1 Kgs 1; 2 Kgs 11; cf. Pss 2, 110). Occasions of national defeat and victory also gave opportunity for worship gatherings (cf. Pss 18, 20–21, 44, 89). The use of psalms in worship is dramatically depicted in 1 Chron 15:1–16:36 (cf. 1 Sam 6), which describes David's procession of the ark to Jerusalem, accompanied by "shouting" and various musical instruments (15:28). At the conclusion of the procession, once the ark is settled in its place, praises are sung, led by "Asaph and his kindred" (16:7). What they sing are, ostensibly, excerpts from Psalms 95, 105–106 (1 Chron 16:8-34). Another example is found in Jeremiah's prophecy of a restored Judah (Jer 33:10-11), when thanksgiving offerings will once again be brought to the temple, accompanied by the words of Ps 136:1.[24]

In addition to the centralized temple, the village, clan, and household constituted *bona fide* communities of faith and ritual. Within these smaller settings, "small-group rituals" were conducted under the guidance of a "ritual expert."[25] The setting of worship (or "cultic" setting) in ancient Israel thus extended beyond the centralized, corporate context of the temple, the place for the "great congregation."[26] Cultic settings also involved the individual: paying tithes at the temple (Deut 26), fulfilling special vows and presenting special offerings (Gen 28:18-22; 2 Sam 5:7-9; Lev 7:16), rendering thanksgiving for recovery from illness (Isa 38:9-20), seeking asylum or refuge in the sanctuary (Deut 19:1-13; 1 Kgs 1:49-53; 2:28-35), resolving legal disputes that involved taking an oath of innocence and relying upon God's verdict (1 Kgs 8:31-32; Num 5:5-31), and seeking forgiveness for a variety of sins (Lev 4:1-6:7). The wide variety of cultic occasions featured in biblical instruction and narrative seems to overlap significantly with the diversity and scope of the Psalter. Many of the psalms were, no doubt, composed and used for cultic performance, both corporate and individual. Others, however, we cannot be sure. For example, the complaint-petitions that populate the Psalter: were they performed in the presence of a priestly intermediary or recited by the supplicant alone, say, in the privacy of his or her home?

Lack of direct evidence has not prevented interpreters from imagining various cultic scenarios that might have pressed the Psalms into active service. The greatest champion of the Psalter's cultic character was the Norwegian scholar Sigmund Mowinckel (1884–1965), well known for his attempt at reconstructing a particular psalm's "cultic situation" with its attendant "liturgical complexity."[27] Mowinckel insisted that most psalms had their home in "the midst of the Great Assembly."[28] In so doing, Mowinckel attempted to reconstruct the rich choreography of First Temple worship.

As part of his clarion call for a cult-centered hermeneutic, Mowinckel devoted near-singular concentration on the autumnal New Year's festival, set within the Festival of Tabernacles. This central festival served as the occasion not just for the enthronement psalms, whose festal shout Mowinckel translated in a uniquely dramatic way ("Yahweh has become king!"), but for much of the Psalter as a whole. Regardless of whether he was correct,[29] Mowinckel demonstrated that the work of worship in ancient Israel, indeed throughout the ancient Near East, was meant to be transformative: reality is shaped by the liturgical act. A "new song" matches a new reality.[30]

As the scope of Israel's "cult" has been significantly enlarged and nuanced in biblical scholarship, so also has been the concept of "life setting." Building on Mowinckel's treatment of the cult, Walter Brueggemann has widened the concept of "function" and "cult" in ways that make the Psalms readily accessible to, indeed performable for, modern readers. For Brueggemann, the cult, irrespective of its ancient ceremonial dynamics, is a world-creating drama. By broadening the scope of the psalmic *Sitz*, Brueggemann classifies the Psalms in three broad categories: orientation, disorientation, and new orientation.[31] The first includes the psalms of descriptive praise (à la Westermann); the second consists of complaint-petitions; and the third comprises psalms of declarative praise (or "thanksgiving"). With these three categories,

Brueggemann offers a typology of psalmic movement that coheres with and drives the life of faith, in which the transition to new orientation inevitably entails struggle and protest. All in all, the performative nature of the Psalms keeps the idea of genre fluid and flexible, from the choreography of ancient worship to the more generalized settings of suffering and joy. In any case, the Psalms continue to "perform," shaping the life of faith amid the traumas and triumphs of life *coram deo*.

Meditatio

Finally, the Psalms' performative power draws not only from the practices of ancient worship. There is, in addition, a fundamental activity referenced in the first psalm that orients the reader to the rest of the Psalter.

> Happy is the one who neither walks in the advice of the
> wicked,
>> nor stands in the path of sinners,
>>> nor sits in the assembly of scoffers;
>> but instead finds delight in YHWH's *tôrâ*,
>>> meditating (*yehgeh*) on his *tôrâ* day and night. (1:1-2)

The common English translation of "meditate" (so NRSV and NIV) draws from the Vulgate *meditabitur*. The Hebrew, however, carries a wider range of meaning, from *moan* and *growl* to *speak* and *consider*, covering everything from the inarticulate to the articulate.[32] Most commonly in the Psalms, the verb in Hebrew (*hgh*) designates human discourse:

> The mouth of the righteous will *utter* wisdom;
>> his tongue will speak justice. (37:30)

> Then my tongue shall *proclaim* your righteousness
>> and your praise all day long. (35:28)

> Those who seek my harm *speak* of ruin,
>> all day long. (38:12)

With the tongue or mouth frequently as its subject, the verb bears a distinctly discursive nuance (see also 115:7). This is also evident in its relevant nominal forms:

My mouth shall speak wisdom;
  the discourse (*hāgût*) of my heart is understanding.
                                        (49:3)

May the words of my mouth
  and the discourse (*hegyôn*) of my heart
be acceptable to you, YHWH,
  my rock and my redeemer. (19:14)

In both instances, mouth and heart are set in parallel positions, along with speech and "discourse." Curiously, in its verbal form *hgh* most often refers to the mouth, but in its nominal forms its most frequent antecedent subject is "heart." Psalm 19 is particularly significant, for the last verse marks the entire psalm as the speaker's discourse ("meditation") of both the "mouth" and "heart" offered to YHWH (cf. synonymous terminology in 104:34). Here, "meditation" takes on an active, creative, distinctly discursive sense. It designates the crafting of poetry, the shaping of psalms, offered to God.

And so we return to Psalm 1. Some have suggested that the verb in verse 2 means "read in an undertone" or "murmur." But that is far too understated in light of the active, wide-ranging sense the verb and its nominal forms carry elsewhere in the Psalms. If an entire psalm can be the product of one's "meditation," as we find in Psalm 19, then "meditation" in Psalm 1 may refer to the creative process of poetic discourse that constitutes the Psalter itself. Psalm 1, in other words, claims the Psalter as the tangible, performative result of "meditation," the *poesis* of the community of faith. As we have seen, reading poetry, ancient or modern, is no passive exercise.[33] It is akin to creating poetry, and reading the Psalms is no exception. It itself is an act of *meditatio*.

CHAPTER 5

PSALMS AS COLLECTIONS AND CLUSTERS

As the most extensive book of the Bible, Psalms is also the most complex. The Psalter is not simply a vast collection of psalms; it is, more accurately, a vast collection of collections and clusters of psalms. Like stars set in their various constellations, most of the 150 psalms are embedded in numerous arrangements and collections, both large and small, some haphazard and others tightly organized. To put it another way, no psalm is an island; each is part of an archipelago or network of psalms that surround it. How these networks inform our interpretation of Psalms is the subject of this chapter.

The Complexity of Collections

One might expect, or at least hope, that the psalms of the Psalter would be organized according to genre: all the complaint-petitions, for example, would be grouped together in one corner, the thanksgiving songs grouped in another, with the royal psalms and praise hymns located within their own tidy, discrete collections. Not so, however. From start to finish, there is plenty of

generic intermixing to go around in the Psalter.[1] Although we can
discern certain kinds of collections, they are not, for the most part,
determined by genre.[2] Instead, such collections are identified by
their superscriptions, as listed below:

Davidic collection(s)	3–41; 51–71(72); 108–110; 138–145
Korahite collection(s)	42–49; 84–85; 87–88
Asaphite collection	(50) 73–83

Although none of them is self-contained, these "collections" are
defined by their common associations with particular persons.
Each psalm within these collections bears a superscription or title
that attributes it to a person or persons. Most prominent is David,
whose name appears in nearly half of the psalms of the Psalter (73
total). The other "personal" collections include that of the
Korahites ("sons of Korah")—a guild of temple singers, gatekeep-
ers, and bakers[3]—and that of Asaph, a temple singer who was
appointed by David to oversee music performed in worship and
who sang at the dedication of Solomon's temple.[4]

Other psalms, however, bear no such pedigree but are united
instead by common theme or literary distinction.

Elohistic collection	42–83
Enthronement hymns	47, 93, 95–99
Songs of ascents	120–134
Hallelujah psalms	111–117, 146–150

The so-called Elohistic collection includes three other collections:
portions of the Korahite and Davidic collections, as well as all of
the Asaphite psalms. Its defining feature is a distinct yet inconsis-
tently applied preference for "God" (*'ĕlôhîm*) over "LORD"
(*YHWH*) in reference to the deity.[5] Lacking superscriptions, the
enthronement hymns are united by content and style, making
them a "thematic grouping" rather than a collection.[6] Together,
they celebrate God's kingship over Israel and the nations with the
resounding proclamation, "YHWH is king!" (Pss 93:1; 96:10; 97:1;
99:1). The songs of ascents, a more diverse group, are distinguished by their unique superscription *šîr hamma'ălôt*, perhaps
designating their use as pilgrimage songs. The two groupings of
hallelujah psalms, along with one "stray" psalm (135), include
psalms of thanksgiving and praise, many of which open with the
command to praise. Each of the last five psalms is bracketed by
the command *hallelujah*, providing a fitting conclusion to the

Psalter. In addition to the larger collections, Psalms 52–55 bear the common title *maskîl* ("wisdom song"). The superscriptions of Psalms 56–60 contain the word *miktām* ("inscription").

There are, however, many psalms that fall outside these various corpora. They include the following:

Psalm 86	"A Prayer of David."
Psalm 89	"A *maskîl* of Ethan the Ezrahite."
Psalm 90	"A Prayer of Moses, the man of God."
Psalm 92	"A Psalm: A Song for the Sabbath Day."
Psalm 101	"Of David. A Psalm."
Psalm 102	"The Prayer of One Afflicted, When Faint, as He Pours Out His Petition before YHWH."
Psalm 103	"Of David."

Psalms 89 and 90 are genuine "outsiders," since their pedigree is nowhere else attested in the Psalter.[7] But even outsiders need some company: Moses and Ethan, perhaps not coincidentally, are canonically tied together. Psalms 92 and 102, however, exhibit no personal ascription. The three relatively lone psalms ascribed to David (86, 101, 103) are either secondary to the larger Davidic corpus (3–72) or are splinters from it. Perhaps they are "stray" psalms that became situated in their relatively lone positions for a specific reason. One of them, for example, splits the Korah collection in half (86), while a small group of three Davidic psalms (108–110) separates a cluster of praise psalms (104–107) from a group of hallelujah psalms (111–117).

Several psalms lack superscriptions entirely; they are the "orphans" of the Psalter. They include 1–2, 10, 43, 91, 104–107, 118, 119, 136–137. At least two, however, are untitled extensions of previous psalms: Psalms 10 and 43. Psalms 1 and 2, in addition, bear no superscription, and hence do not figure in the Davidic collection that follows. Together, they serve as the ostensible introduction to the Psalter as a whole.

Sample Collections

Collections, clusters, strays, outsiders, and orphans: all make for a rather motley and complex corpus we call the Psalter. But whether they hold membership in a major collection or lie "outside," all the psalms are placed where they are, and each one has its surrounding neighbors, thereby sharing certain hermeneutical affinities. That is to say, by being placed together, these psalms have the opportunity to "talk" to one another; they become dialogically engaged as we read them sequentially in their juxtaposed positions.[8] The following discussion is devoted to understanding something about the collective dialogue within four discrete collections and one smaller cluster or group.

David under Duress

Psalms attributed to David comprise the largest collection, or collections, dispersed from Psalms 3 to 145. The preposition *lĕ* in the superscription could refer specifically to authorship ("of" or "by" David) or to some broader kind of relationship between David and the psalm so titled (e.g., "for," "about," "after the manner of," or "dedicated to" David). The precise nuance of the preposition is widely debated, and complicating the discussion is the fact that the superscriptions are secondary to the psalms they preface, offering precious little evidence that the psalms were actually written by Israel's most famous king. Several of the psalms attributed to David, for example, make clear reference to the temple,[9] which according to biblical lore was built not by David but by his son Solomon (1 Kgs 5–8). The double superscription of Psalm 30 is particularly curious: "A Psalm <A Dedicatory Song for the Temple> of David."[10] However, David is remembered in biblical lore for his abilities as a gifted musician and composer,[11] as much as Solomon is known for his wisdom,[12] which would make David a powerful magnet for psalmic attribution.

Just as the historical question of these psalms is left open, so also is the issue about the exact meaning of the Davidic superscriptions. Regardless of the psalms' actual authorship, the Davidic superscriptions could suggest implied authorship. At the very least, the editors responsible for adding the psalmic titles determined that these psalms were best read with reference to David, as if they had been written by him, for him, or with him in mind. In any case, David's voice, the superscriptions claim, rings loud and clear throughout the collection. David becomes the prime performer of these psalms, as is evident in the more detailed superscriptions that reference particular events in David's life.[13] If not autobiographical, such psalms exhibit a distinctly biographical dimension. These superscriptions, with David cast as the superscriptional subject of these psalms, add a new layer of interpretation.

Beyond their poetic and form-critical dimensions, these psalms *qua* Davidic psalms invite readers to interpret them with David in mind, to fill out his character, even to identify with him. The anguished and ecstatic words that fill every strophe identify David as the supreme model of prayer and praise for every reader. Ultimately, the collection bears a distinctly pastoral function. To use these psalms as if David performed them grants every reader a measure of David's sufferings and triumphs. By reciting these psalms, readers take on David's own voice and, by adopting his words, are "Davidized," that is, they become associated with Israel's most beloved (and troubled) king. As much as these psalms humanize, indeed "democratize," David, as some would say, they also elevate readers, bringing them into the covenantal circle of intimacy between David and his God.

So what do these psalms reveal about David? They articulate before God and at the level of public disclosure his anguish and joy, his prayer and praise. To draw from Psalms 3–41 and 51–72 by way of illustration, we find an overwhelming concentration of prayers for deliverance from enemies, iniquities, and illnesses. They paint a vivid picture of David under duress. The opening psalm of the collection complains, "YHWH, how numerous are my foes!" (3:1). Enemies, both external and familial, beset the Davidic speaker (e.g., 17:9; 55:12). This David is victimized and persecuted; he counts himself among the afflicted and oppressed (9:12-13; 10:12), even godforsaken (22:1). He identifies himself as "poor and needy" (40:17=70:5; cf. 9:18). The vivid yet stereotypical descriptions of distress and deprivation provide a defining backdrop for the enduring bond David shares with God. Read with the superscriptions, the prayers and praises reveal David's deep piety. Consider again the opening Davidic psalm: "I cry out to YHWH, and from his holy hill he answers me" (3:3). And on the other side of distress: "Because your benevolence is better than life itself, my lips will praise you" (63:3).

The human-divine relationship represented by David and God in these psalms is cast in various metaphors: God is David's strength, fortress, shield, refuge, and rock, images that are dispersed throughout the collection but are also uniquely concentrated in the opening lines of Psalm 18, a royal psalm (vv. 1-2; cf. 31:1-4; 71:3). The intimacy David shares with God is captured well in the following verses:

YHWH, my choice portion and my cup;
    you hold my lot. (16:5)

Guard me as the apple of the eye;
    conceal me in the shadow of your wings. (17:8)

Indeed, you light my lamp, YHWH;
    my God illumines my darkness. (18:28)

YHWH is my shepherd, I lack nothing. (23:1)

YHWH is my strength and my shield;
    in him my heart trusts;
I was helped, and my heart exulted,
    and with my song I give him thanks.
YHWH is the strength of his people;
    he is a saving refuge for his anointed. (28:7-8)

See, God is my helper;
    the Lord is the one who sustains my life. (54:4)

The personal bond between David and God is established not only by God's benevolence and mercy (e.g., 5:7; 6:4; 13:5; 17:7; 63:3; 69:16). The speaker is adamant that his own integrity has solicited God's favor:

YHWH rewarded me for my righteousness;
    for the cleanness of my hands he restored me.
                    (18:20 [see v. 24])

YHWH will judge the peoples;
    judge me, YHWH, according to my righteousness,
        according to the integrity within me. (7:8)

Judge me, YHWH, for I have walked in my integrity;
    in YHWH I have put my trust; I have not slipped. (26:1)

> You uphold me in my integrity,
>> and set me before you forever. (41:12)

Lest we get a one-sided picture of David's righteous integrity *vis-à-vis* God, the speaker admits that God's righteousness also plays an essential role:

> Judge me, YHWH, my God, by *your* righteousness. (35:24*a*)

The full picture of David's character becomes more complex as one takes into account the so-called penitential psalms that populate the Davidic collection: Psalms 6, 32, 38, 51 (and 143; see also 102 and 130). In these psalms, the speaker appeals to God's mercy while openly confessing his sin (38:18; 51:1). Psalm 51, whose superscription makes reference to David's affair with Bathsheba (see 2 Sam 11:1–12:23), is the most well known.

> Grant me mercy, O God, according to your benevolence;
>> according to your abundant compassion wipe away my
>>> transgressions.
> Wash me thoroughly of my iniquity;
>> purify me of my sin.
> Indeed, I acknowledge my transgressions;
>> my sin is ever before me.
> Against you, you alone, have I sinned;
>> I have committed what is evil in your sight,
> So that you are just when you speak,
>> pure when you pass judgment.
> Indeed, I was born in iniquity;
>> my mother conceived me in sin. (51:1-7)

> Hide your face from my sins,
>> and wipe away all my wrongdoings.
> Create in me a clean heart, O God,
>> and renew within me a steadfast spirit.
> Do not cast me out from your presence;
>> do not take your holy spirit from me.
> . . . .
> Deliver me from bloody violence, O God,
>> the God of my salvation,
>>> so that my tongue shall sing aloud
>>> of your righteousness.

O Lord, open my lips,
    that my mouth shall proclaim your praise.
(vv. 9-11, 14-15)

The original ending of the psalm describes the appropriate posture before God, "a broken spirit":

For you do not desire sacrifice;
    were I to offer a burnt offering, you would not accept it.
My sacrifice, O God, is a broken spirit;
    a broken and crushed heart, O God, you do not despise.
(vv. 16-18)

A "broken and crushed heart" and an inestimable righteousness: David embodies both. This David is a character of extremes, both confident and undone, sinful and righteous, anguished and joyful, but ultimately showing unwavering trust in God, his deliverer: "Deliverance belongs to YHWH" (3:8). As much as he beseeches God for instruction ("teach me your paths" [25:4]), David also exhorts his audience: "Come, O children, and listen to me; / Let me teach you the fear of YHWH" (34:11). The David figured in these psalms is a man for all seasons.

The final psalm of the collection, Psalm 72, titled "Of Solomon," outlines the king's responsibility to uphold and administer justice.

O God, give the king your judgments,
    and your righteousness to the king's son.
May he judge your people with righteousness,
    and your poor with justice.
May the mountains yield *shalom* for the people,
    and the hills (yield) righteousness.
May he defend the poor of the people,
    save the children of the needy,
        and crush the oppressor. (72:1-4)

Maintaining justice, according to the psalm, is the king's paramount task. For a postexilic people bereft of a native king, the Davidic psalms do not simply recall the glories and troubles of the monarchic past; they apply themselves to the present for each and every reader. The king's responsibility is everyone's. Furthermore, the Davidic psalms in particular come to express the community's hope for a new king, a Messiah who would restore Israel. Through the psalms, the royal David of the past becomes the prototype of the future.[14]

92

Korah in Sanctuary and Sheol

To the "sons of Korah" are attributed eleven psalms (42 and 43 form a single psalm), which together contain some of the most poignant imagery and heightened pathos found anywhere in the Psalter. The collection opens with the image of a doe thirsting for streams of water (42:1) and concludes with dark despair engulfing the speaker (88:10). This motley collection consists of two series that exhibit similar movement: the opening of both Psalms 42 and 84 waxes poignantly about the soul's deep desire for God, "the living God" (42:1-2; 84:2). The concluding psalms, 49 and 88, by contrast, dwell on Sheol. Sheol, or the "grave," is the destiny of the rich and foolhardy, but evidently not of the speaker (49:14-15). The last psalm, however, finds the speaker practically, if not figuratively, in Sheol and completely in despair (88:3-6, 10-12).

Within these two somewhat parallel panels, numerous evocative images of God, temple, and city appear. In the first panel, God is depicted as king (44:4; 47:2, 6-8), and in one striking instance, the earthly king is addressed as "God" in a royal wedding litany (45:6). But it is actually Zion, God's earthly abode, that takes center stage in these psalms. As foreign kings conspire to lay siege against Zion, it is the city (not God's anointed) that puts them to flight (48:4-7; cf. 2:1-9). As Israel's "refuge and strength," God dwells in the city, "the holy habitation of the Most High," ensuring its security (46:1, 4-5). As the theological cousin to Psalm 46, Psalm 48 lifts up "the city of the great King" as God's "sure defense" against enemies (vv. 2-3) and offers a virtual tour of Zion, including its towers, ramparts, and citadels (vv. 12-14). Zion, here, is identified "in the far north" (v. 2), suggestive perhaps of a northern origin for the Korahite psalms, which came to be "Zionized" in subsequent compositional and redactional work (see also 42:6-7). In a fit of theological fervor, the psalmist points to Zion and exuberantly proclaims "that this is God" (v. 14). With Psalm 47, an enthronement psalm,[15] sandwiched in between, Psalms 46–48 paint a powerful scene of God enthroned in Zion, protecting the city and guaranteeing its welfare.

The centrality of God's home is an image carried forward into Psalm 84, which compares God's "house" to a nest for the swallow or sparrow (v. 3). Zion is not only the habitat for divinity; it is home for all. It is no coincidence that Psalm 84 contains the most references to "happiness" of any psalm in the Psalter (84:4, 5, 12).

It marks the joyous fulfillment of Psalms 42 and 43 (esp. 42:4-5; 43:2-4). Whereas the speaker in Psalms 42 and 43 walks about despondently, yearning to enter God's "dwelling" (43:2-3), Psalm 84 speaks as if from the sanctuary itself, equating "happiness" with dwelling in God's "house" (v. 4) and trusting in God (v. 12). Whereas the speaker in Psalm 42 wonders whether beholding God's face will ever happen again (vv. 2-3), the speaker in Psalm 84 proclaims resolutely that "the God of gods will be seen in Zion" (v. 7). Psalm 87 proclaims that, of all of "Jacob's dwellings," Zion is God's favorite (v. 2). It is there, the birthplace of a chosen and protected people, that God registers God's own (v. 6).

The final psalm of the collection, however, returns to the despondency of Psalms 42 and 43, and with a vengeance. The depths of death, the "Pit," replace the holy mount. Sheol and the shades displace the summit of God's holy presence. Whereas the temple is the place to "ponder [God's] *hesed*," or benevolence (48:9), the grave is utterly devoid of God's "benevolence" and "faithfulness" (88:11). Together, the psalms of the "sons of Korah" take the reader to the majestic heights of Zion and to the harrowing depths of Sheol. According to priestly lore, Korah himself, the eponymous ancestor of this group of temple singers, descended to Sheol as punishment for his rebellion against Aaron and Moses (Num 16:31-34). Such a stained legacy may have shaped the movement of this collection, concluding it with the most depressing psalm of the Psalter. Psalm 88, in other words, could be Korah's signature psalm.

Asaph before God

Like the Korahite psalms that surround them, the Psalms of Asaph constitute a small collection—twelve to be exact. Indeed, the Asaphite psalms complement the Korahite psalms: as the latter stress God's royal nature, the former lifts up God as judge over all the nations. It is no surprise, then, that the Asaphite collection contains the highest concentration of divine discourse in the Psalter (see 50:5, 7-15, 16-23; 75:2-5, 10; 81:6-16; 82:2-4, 6-7). God consistently speaks in judgment or admonition. God calls Israel, all the peoples, and even the gods to account (e.g., Pss 50, 76, 81, 82). In Psalm 82, Israel's God judges other members of the divine council for having failed to execute justice for "the weak and the orphan," the "lowly and the destitute," by delivering them from the "hand of the wicked" (82:3-4). They are thus sentenced to death (v. 7). The psalm concludes with an appeal to God to judge the earth and its nations (v. 8). As God has done in heaven, so God shall do on earth, the psalmist hopes.

The opening psalm of the collection, Psalm 50, sets the tone for the entire corpus: as judge, God admonishes Israel, specifically for not offering sacrifices in the spirit of thanksgiving (50:4, 6). God does not need the sacrifice of animals, as if God were hungry for flesh and blood (vv. 12-13). Rather, God requires from worshipers "thanksgiving as their sacrifice" (v. 23). Psalm 50 elucidates the nature of thanksgiving:

> Present to God a sacrifice of thanksgiving,
>   and pay to *Elyon* your vows.
> Call upon me on the day of distress;
>   I will deliver you so that you shall glorify me. (vv. 14-15)

Whether an actual ceremonial sacrifice is meant here is debatable, but in any case, a right sacrifice is more reflective of the worshiper's disposition before God than of God's actual need. The condition and purpose of sacrifice is clarified in verse 15: thanksgiving is the petitioner's response to answered prayer, the response that "glorifies" God. In Psalm 50, God has identified thanksgiving as the definitive way of honoring God in response to God's salvific work (v. 23).

Calling upon God for deliverance and acknowledging God's salvific work are the two performative poles of this collection. On the one hand, the Asaphite psalms include several prayers for deliverance and restoration on behalf of the distressed community whose temple is destroyed (Pss 74, 79, 80, 83). On the other hand, God's mighty deeds are gratefully recounted (73:28; 77:11; 78:4). The Asaphite collection includes, not coincidentally, Psalm 78, a historical psalm that recounts God's "glorious deeds" and "wonders" (v. 4) while also highlighting Israel's stubborn ingratitude (see also 81:10-16). Deliverance from enemies and sustenance in the wilderness are the hallmarks of God's salvific work (78:19-20, 23-29; 81:10, 16). Thankful praise and obedience are what God expects, not rebellion and ingratitude. Hence, Psalm 75, the one thanksgiving psalm in the collection, offers a model for rendering thanksgiving to God that also includes an admonition from God (vv. 2-5).

Journeying Home: The Songs of Ascents

Each of these fifteen psalms bears the enigmatic superscription *šîr hammaʻălôt,* "the song of ascents," which might refer to the "ascent" made by pilgrims to Jerusalem, perhaps to attend one of the three major festivals (see 122:4). Several of the psalms point to Jerusalem or Zion as a point of destination or as the center of activity. "I rejoiced with those who said to me, 'Let us go to YHWH's house!'" (122:1). Zion is also God's destination (132:2, 7, 13-14) and the locus of blessing for God's people (122:9; 125:2; 128:5; 134:3). "All who hate Zion" are to be "turned back" (129:5). The call for peace and prosperity for Israel and Jerusalem resounds throughout the collection (122:6; 125:5; 128:5-6; cf. 120:7). Psalm 133 celebrates the unity of community with the evocative images of holy oil and dew. The "mountains of Zion" are where YHWH has "ordained his blessing" (v. 3).

Speaking of mountains: Psalm 125 likens those who "trust in YHWH" to Mount Zion, which itself is surrounded by mountains "as YHWH surrounds his people" (vv. 1-2). The speaker of Psalm 121 lifts his or her eyes "to the hills" to determine the true source of help, which is YHWH, "who made heaven and earth" (vv. 1-2). Psalm 123 commends lifting the eyes to the one "enthroned in the heavens" (v. 1). Hands are lifted to "the holy place," to YHWH, "maker of heaven and earth," in Zion (134:2-3). Ascent, thus, takes on various forms in these psalms.

But there is one notable counterpoint to this language of ascent: taking a more personal and poignant turn, the speaker of Psalm 131 avoids raising his or her eyes "too high"; instead, he or she lifts up a "calmed and quieted" soul, likened to a "weaned child with its mother" (v. 2), as the proper posture before God. Familial imagery also pervades Psalms 127–128, which commend a prosperous home: for example, a man's "quiver full of [sons]" and a wife as "a fruitful vine" (127:3-5; 128:3-5). But intertwined in these complementary psalms is an urgent concern for Israel's welfare (127:1*b*, 5*b*; 128:5-6). Even the most intimate psalm in the collection concludes with a mandate that Israel "hope in YHWH" (131:3). The domestic theme, moreover, also pertains to the God of David. According to Psalm 132, YHWH "desired Zion...for his residence" (v. 13). Zion is God's "resting place" (v. 14). In these psalms, home is habitat for divinity as well as for humanity.

Peace for all Israel, Zion's restoration, prosperity of the home, and personal protection: all are bound together in these evocative psalms. Regardless of whether they were actually used by pilgrims on their way to Jerusalem, these psalms transport the reader to the source of *shalom*—individual, familial, and national. They offer an ascent, a destination, to the fount of all blessing.

A Literary Cluster: Psalms 15–24

And now for a "collection" of a completely different sort. As part of the larger Davidic collection, Psalms 15–24 exhibit a remarkably well-crafted arrangement. These ten psalms constitute a highly organized cluster or grouping,[16] reflecting a sophisticated level of editorial organization. In this arrangement, each psalm is tightly related to another and to the group as a whole.

This cluster of psalms features a distinctly chiastic arrangement, as defined in part by the various genres represented therein:

A Psalm 15 (entrance liturgy)
   B   Psalm 16 (song of trust)
       C   Psalm 17 (complaint-petition)
           D   Psalm 18 (royal psalm)
               E   Psalm 19 (Torah psalm)
           D'   Psalms 20–21 (royal psalms)
       C'   Psalm 22 (complaint-petition)
   B' Psalm 23 (song of trust)
A' Psalm 24 (entrance liturgy)

In a chiastic arrangement, the reader's attention is directed to what is outermost and to what is innermost, or central. In this case, the entrance liturgies (Pss 15 and 24) suggest that the organization is more than simply concentric. Because both psalms make reference to God's "holy mountain" or "hill" (15:1; 24:3), the overall arrangement of this cluster takes on a distinctly metaphorical shape, with Psalm 19 assuming the "summit" of the arrangement.

```
                    Psalm 19
            Psalm 18        Psalms 20–21
      Psalm 17                    Psalm 22
   Psalm 16                            Psalm 23
Psalm 15                                    Psalm 24
```

Psalm 19, thus, is the "king of the hill," positioned to govern this cluster of psalms hermeneutically, even as the surrounding psalms support or complement it in various ways. The concentric arrangement gives rise, not fortuitously, to a literary configuration shaped by ascent and descent. Or, to put it another way, all the psalms, except for the one on top, "build up" in various ways to Psalm 19. Together, Psalms 15–24 form a theological "tell," whose horizontal and vertical cross sections reveal an abundance of layered connections, a sampling of which is discussed below.

At the Foothills: Psalms 15 and 24

That Psalms 15 and 24 have to do with admission into God's "holy place" is indicated by their similar questions:

> YHWH, who shall lodge in your tent?
> Who shall dwell on your holy mountain? (15:1)

> Who shall ascend YHWH's hill?
> And who shall stand in his holy place? (24:3)

The site of destination is variously described as a mountain and a hill, a tent and a holy place. Admission, likewise, is variously described as dwelling, lodging, ascending, and standing.

Both psalms have as their centerpiece certain moral qualifications for admission (15:2-5*a*; 24:4), which, in relation to the central Psalm 19, are folded into the rubric of *tôrâ* (19:7-10). The entrance qualifications of these outer psalms are, in effect, counted among God's precepts and ordinances referenced in 19:8-10. They not only allow for admission into the temple; they are also deemed life-giving and of ultimate desire in their own right (v. 11). All in all, Psalms 15, 19, and 24 share in common the supreme value of right conduct, specifically *tôrâ* piety, and its salutary consequences (cf. 15:5*b*; 24:5; 19:8-10).

The profile of God in Psalm 24, moreover, finds peculiar resonance with Psalm 19. The divine warrior, "YHWH strong and mighty...in war" (24:8*b*), by approaching and entering through the temple gates, traces a path comparable to that of the sun described in Psalm 19:

> For the sun, [God] has set a tent in the heavens.
> It is like a bridegroom
> going forth from his wedding canopy;

> it rejoices like a warrior (*gibbôr*)
> running the path. (19:4*b*-5)

A "tent" is established as a solar residence, from which the sun goes forth at the break of dawn. As the divine warrior *enters* his residence after battle, the solar warrior *exits* his residence after the night (to reenter, of course, at the end of the day). Such complementarity of movement establishes a deep connection between solar entity and military deity: the sun's daily trek is a victory tour, and the divine warrior is imbued with solar attributes.

Psalms 19 and 24 also share the theme of divine glory. As the cosmos declares God's glory (19:2), so those who seek God's "face" bear witness to the King of glory (24:7-10). Human and celestial agents are united in common testimony. Creation, moreover, figures significantly in the opening of Psalm 24, just as it does in Psalm 19. In both psalms, cosmos and instruction are conjoined. All the earth belongs to YHWH (24:1). Divine ownership is grounded in God's founding the earth upon the seas (v. 2). By association, YHWH's "hill" or "holy place" constitutes a microcosm of the well-established earth. To ascend it is, in effect, to scale the pinnacle of creation. Zion displays the creator's glory as much as the cosmos above bears witness to it. The holy summit becomes a celestial observatory from which to witness, day and night, the silent testimony of the heavens to God's glory.

From Trust to Torah: Psalms 16 and 23

Psalms 16 and 23 mark the next "step" in the chiastic ascent. United by the common themes of protection and provision, both psalms delineate the contours of trust and well-being. Psalm 16, in particular, addresses the issue of allegiance to YHWH. The speaker declares at the outset that he or she has taken "refuge in" God (v. 1*b*) and that the source of the speaker's well-being is found only in YHWH (v. 2). The speaker, moreover, acknowledges YHWH as the source of instruction (v. 7).[17] Indeed, from God the very "path of life" is revealed (v. 11). In fulfillment of 15:5, the speaker declares that he or she will not be "shaken" (16:8*b*). The speaker is protected from Sheol, the antithesis of God's "holy hill" (v. 10).

Psalm 23, too, describes the blessed life of trust in and provision by God. The pastoral imagery of Psalm 23 matches the property imagery of Psalm 16. In both, divine provision precludes all lack (23:1; 16:2*b*).

PSALMS

In Psalm 16, the speaker delights in the *stationary* property of land, while the speaker of Psalm 23 celebrates being part of YHWH's *movable* property, as a sheep cared for by its shepherd. The shift in perspective from Psalm 16 to 23 is apt: from the speaker's property to God's property. In Psalm 23, the speaker belongs wholly to God, as much as the speaker's property in Psalm 16 belongs to him or her as given by God (cf. 24:1). Divine instruction in 16:7 takes on the graphic form of the shepherd's guiding "rod" and "staff," symbols also of protection amid danger (23:4*b*). The "path of life" in 16:11 follows the "paths of righteousness" in 23:3. The familial context of Psalm 16 reemerges in Psalm 23, wherein pastoral vistas give way to the household table setting. The cup apportioned by God in 16:5 is well filled in 23:5. It is in such a familial context that enemies are also at the table, with "goodness" and "benevolence" replacing the enemies as the speaker's "pursuers" (vv. 5-6).

With its broad focus on *tôrâ*, Psalm 19 ensures that these two songs of trust are taken prescriptively. As *tôrâ* is "complete" or "whole" (19:8*a*), so the one who trusts in God suffers "no lack" (23:1). YHWH's instruction mentioned in 16:7 is formalized in *tôrâ*, which imparts "wisdom to the simple" (19:8*b*). As the speaker of Psalm 16 is instructed "at night" (v. 7), so "night" imparts knowledge of God (19:3*b*). Trust and *tôrâ* are bound together; so also joy. The joy that accompanies trust and instruction, stressed particularly in Psalm 16, is associated with the sun's "running the path" in 19:6. The image of the exuberant sun is linked with the individual who follows the path of righteousness and, thus, obeys *tôrâ* (19:10*b*). Borne of trust, the individual's joy becomes cosmically effulgent, which, like the sun's light, dispels the darkness of valleys (19:8; 23:4).

From Petition to Praise: Psalms 17 and 22

Out of trust comes petition, and from petition comes vindication. Psalm 22 refers to the ancestors' well-placed trust in God's saving power as precedent for the speaker's urgent petition (vv. 5-6). In the opening lines of Psalm 17, the supplicant twice describes his or her own integrity, particularly of the mouth (vv. 3, 4), as warrant for petition (see also 15:2*b*-3*a*), and confidently claims his or her unwavering trek on divinely prescribed paths (17:5*b*; cf. 16:11; 23:3). The speaker's particular petition is for "refuge from adversaries" (17:7), for concealment in the "shadow of [YHWH's]

100

wings" (v. 8*b*). The speaker's enemies pursue and surround him or her (v. 11); collectively, they act like a rapacious "lion" (v. 12).

The lion featured in Psalm 17 is accompanied by other dangerous animals in Psalm 22, including dogs and bulls, all metaphors for the speaker's enemies (vv. 13-14, 21*b*, 22), all surrounding the speaker (vv. 13, 17), as they do in Psalm 17 (v. 11*a*). Consonant with the common theme of enemies is the genre that unites these two psalms. Petition, not coincidentally, also plays a crucial role at the conclusion of Psalm 19.

> Who can discern (my) errors?
> From hidden sins clear me!
> Even from the insolent (*zēdîm*)[18] deliver your servant;
> let them not gain mastery over me.
> Then I will become entirely blameless,
> and innocent of great transgression. (vv. 12-13)

The surrounding enemies so vividly described in Psalms 17 and 22 are subsumed under the category of the "insolent" in Psalm 19. The "insolent" threaten to gain mastery over the speaker. Psalm 22 describes in particularly graphic terms the traumatic nature of such mastery: the speaker is held in derision (vv. 7-9), overpowered (vv. 13, 17), wasting away (vv. 15-16*a*), and on the brink of death (v. 16*b*). Psalm 17 complains of enemies poised to "bend [the speaker] to the ground" (v. 11*b*). With the addition and placement of Psalm 19 in this network of psalms, enemy and iniquity become juxtaposed, if not collapsed altogether. In any case, both are deemed impediments to the individual's integrity.

The focus on the sun in Psalm 19 finds subtle connection with the imagery in the complaint-petition psalms. At the conclusion of Psalm 17, YHWH's deliverance is associated with the morning:

> I myself will behold your countenance in righteousness;
> I shall be satisfied when I awake (before) your likeness.
> (v. 15)

The final colon alludes to the speaker's awakening, the occasion of which YHWH's salvation, or display of *ḥesed*, is encountered. God's "likeness" is compared to the dawn. In light of its superscription, Psalm 22 is also associated, in some fashion, with the morning: "according to the 'Doe of the Dawn.'" The dawn serves as the metaphorical occasion for deliverance from danger.

Indeed, Psalm 22 pleads that God "make haste" to the speaker's aid (v. 20*b*), matching the sun's energetic circuit across the sky in Psalm 19 (vv. 6-8). Read together, these two complaint psalms endow the solar imagery of Psalm 19 with soteriological force. The salvific in-breaking of YHWH's effulgent presence is routinized by the sun's daily heliophany and personalized in the regular reading of *tôrâ* (see also Ps 1).

Finally, the language of praise that concludes Psalm 22 finds correspondence with the opening of Psalm 19. The speaker, now delivered, states his or her intent to "declare" YHWH's name to the congregation (v. 23). So also do the heavens "declare God's glory" (19:2). As praise elicited from the speaker's lips extends throughout the congregation and encompasses the "ends of the earth" in recounting YHWH's deeds (22:28), so creation's proclamation of God's glory extends throughout all the earth (19:5) as the sun traverses the celestial dome (v. 7). As the petitioner cries out to God without answer both "day" and "night" (22:3), so day and night render uninterrupted discourse of God's glory to all creation (19:3). In Psalms 19 and 22, continual petition is matched with perennial testimony.

The Ascent to Victory: Psalms 18 and 20–21

The nearest neighbors of Psalm 19 are the royal Psalms 18, 20, and 21. Psalm 18, also a thanksgiving song, appropriately follows the previous psalm of deliverance. The Davidic superscription identifies a particular situation of distress brought about by "all [David's] enemies," including Saul. It opens with an accumulation of metaphors, from refuge and crag to stronghold, rock, horn, and shield, all images of divine protection (v. 3; see also vv. 31*b*, 32*b*, 36*a*, 47*a*). Following this vivid testimony of trust are accounts of the king's distress and victory over his enemies on the battlefield. The king's cry is met with God's response as cosmic warrior, whose theophany is drawn from conventional storm imagery (vv. 8-16). This dramatic scene gives testimony of the king's rescue from the "mighty waters" and the "strong enemy" (vv. 17-20*a*). In the following section, the individual credits his own righteousness as warrant for divine deliverance (vv. 21-25): he has unwaveringly kept to YHWH's "ways" (v. 22) and set YHWH's "statutes" and "ordinances" before him (v. 23), proving integrity (v. 23). Matching the speaker's integrity is God's integrity, which proves faithful and pure (vv. 26-27a), as demonstrated in the deliverance of a "poor people" (v. 28a). The king enumerates a number of ways YHWH has empowered him in battle: YHWH serves as his light (v. 29) and equips him with superhuman strength (vv. 30, 33-37). Deliverance belongs to YHWH (vv. 49-51).

Psalms 20 and 21 are *Zwillingspsalmen,* twins joined at the rhetorical hip. Together, they form an answered petition. Both are spoken primarily by someone other than the king on behalf of the king. Addressing the king, the speaker in Psalm 20 indirectly petitions YHWH to fulfill the king's plans for victory "on the day of distress" (v. 2; cf. 18:19) and appeals for divine help from the "sanctuary," that is, "Zion" (v. 3; see also 18:7b). Opening on a note of joy, Psalm 21 addresses God directly and looks back in thanksgiving at the deliverance wrought by YHWH for the king. The speaker reports that the king rejoices in his deliverance and in YHWH's strength (v. 2). Whereas Psalm 20 requested that YHWH "give to [the king] according to [his] heart" (v. 5a), Psalm 21 declares that the "desire of his heart" has been granted (v. 3a). The king has gained "rich blessings," including a "crown of pure gold" (v. 4), life and length of days (v. 5), majesty and splendor (v. 6b), and "gladness" (v. 7b). On account of his fidelity, the king "will not be shaken" (v. 8b; cf. 15:5b; 16:8b). Continuing to address God, the speaker affirms the certainty of divine victory over the king's enemies (vv. 9-13).

With the placement of Psalm 19 in between these royal psalms, a number of connections are forged. In 18:31, the royal speaker proclaims that YHWH's "word" is "tried and true" (literally, "refined by fire") and that YHWH's "way" is complete or whole, consonant with the character of *tôrâ* described in 19:8-10: "The *tôrâ* of YHWH is whole" (v. 8); "The commandment of YHWH is pure" (v. 9). Indeed, what Psalm 18 says about YHWH's faithful dealings (vv. 26-27a) is comparable to the way *tôrâ* is profiled in 19:8a, 9b, 10a. In Psalm 19, God's integrity is encapsulated in *tôrâ,* the repository of divine favor. Noteworthy, too, are the references to "statutes" and "ordinances" in the center of an *inclusio* in 18:22-24. Together, Psalms 18 and 19 lay claim that God's integrity is reflected in *tôrâ*'s integrity, to be embodied by the individual who does not waver from YHWH's "ways."

Another consonance between Psalm 19 and the royal psalms is the identity of the king. The superscription of Psalm 18 identifies the speaker as David, "YHWH's servant" (v. 1). The speaker of Psalm 19 is identified also as the "servant" of YHWH (19:12a, 14a). More broadly, the three royal psalms serve to "Davidize" not only Psalm 19 but the cluster of psalms as a whole. Consequently, "the ruler and the torah lover...merge into one."[19]

In addition, the king's ability on the battlefield in Psalm 18 finds a particular connection with the image of the sun in Psalm 19. In Psalm 18, the king can "run over a wall" (v. 30a); he is girded with "strength"; his way is "perfect" (v. 33); and his "stride" is "lengthened" (v. 37). Such qualities, among others, establish the king's prowess in combat (see also vv. 34-35). It is, thus, no coincidence that the sun in Psalm 19 is also likened to a "warrior (*gibbôr*) running the path" in joy (v. 5b). In 18:33, the path of integrity is also the path that the king traverses with swift and secure feet (vv. 34, 37). But there is more. The theme of effulgent light is also applied to the king: "It is you who lights my lamp; YHWH, my God, illumines my darkness" (18:29). By association, the personification of the sun in Psalm 19 is given royal characterization. The sun is a warrior from whose heat nothing is hidden (19:7b). The language of theophany in Psalm 18, moreover, is replete with destructive images of light (e.g., vv. 13, 15b). Such language sharpens the sun's power all the more to penetrate all that is hidden.

Psalms 20 and 21, in turn, emphasize the warrior's joy in victory (20:6; 21:2, 7). The theme of joy is prominently displayed in Psalm 19 in association with both the sun and *tôrâ*: the sun "rejoices like a warrior running the path" (v. 6b), and "the precepts of YHWH...gladden the heart" (v. 10). Indeed, Psalm 21 connects such joy with the fulfillment of desire:

> The desire of his heart you have granted him;
>> the request of his lips you have not denied. *Selah*
> For you meet him with rich blessings;
>> you set upon his head a crown of pure gold. (21:2-4)

Retaining the image of gold, Psalm 19 also takes up the language of desire but shifts its object from victory in battle and royal blessings to adherence to *tôrâ*:

> They are more desirable than gold,
>> more than abundant fine gold,
>>> sweeter also than honey,
>>>> the drippings of the honeycomb. (19:10)

Tôrâ far exceeds the value of pure gold. Flanked by royal psalms, Psalm 19 lifts up the theme of *tôrâ* as both a corrective and a complement to the royal desire for power and victory. Everything that the king desires and has gained from YHWH—from gladness to gold—is incorporated into and ultimately exceeded by *tôrâ*. As the ultimate object of desire, *tôrâ* relativizes the royal quest for victory. As in Deuteronomy 17:18-20, the study of *tôrâ* in Psalm 19 becomes the highest, most worthy endeavor, displacing all other goals, royal or otherwise. The speaker of Psalm 19, however, is not limited to the king. Like the sun that goes forth from its "tent" to cover the earth with its light, the speaker of Psalm 19 goes forth from royal identity to become anyone and everyone who walks in the way of *tôrâ*. Even as the royal psalms "Davidize" this cluster, Psalm 19 "democratizes" David.

Finally, the cosmic orientation of Psalm 19 finds correspondence with the transcendent source of deliverance identified in 20:7, YHWH's "holy heaven" (cf. v. 3). The heavens, in their cosmic ordering in Psalm 19, have all but replaced Zion's earthly refuge as the locus of divine deliverance (see 18:7*b*; 20:3). Thus, the heavens' declaring "God's glory" and "handiwork" (19:2) includes bearing witness to the king's rescue from defeat. Divine glory is demonstrated in the king's deliverance, but it is also reflected in cosmic creation.

The Cosmic Torah: Psalm 19

We now reach the "top." Positioned as corresponding genres, Psalms 15–24 "talk" to one another through their myriad corresponding themes and associations. However, given its uniquely elevated position in the cluster, Psalm 19 has the last word by governing the theological significance of the cluster "down below." At the same time, Psalm 19 takes on added nuance from its neighboring psalms. It serves, in short, as both complement and corrective to the collection. The psalm, for example, relativizes all references to the temple. Nowhere is Zion or refuge mentioned in Psalm 19. Whereas Psalms 15 and 24 elucidate the qualifications for gaining entrance into the temple—the portal into God's presence—Psalm 19 offers no earthly entrance. Instead, it points to the celestial horizon, shifting the focus from Zion to the sun's "tent," set in the heavens (vv. 5*b*).

PSALMS

Connections abound between the solar image in Psalm 19, on the one hand, and God (Ps 24) and king (Pss 18, 20, 21), on the other, all triggered by the metaphorical association of sun and warrior. With heat as its weapon, the sun takes up the military traits of both God and king but does so absent the violence of battle. On its daily round, the sun achieves cosmic order without conquest. Dispelling the darkness, it illuminates and warms the earth while providing a cosmic model of piety, an unwavering path run with joy.

In Psalm 19, YHWH is more of a quintessential creator than a consummate warrior. In Psalm 19, there is no explicit king, let alone a militant one. The same can be said of the speaker in Psalm 19: there is nothing distinctly royal about him. Wracked with anxiety over "hidden sins," the speaker welcomes the illuminating power of *tôrâ*. The outward threat of enemies featured in the complaint and royal psalms are internalized in Psalm 19. Deliverance from enemies is transformed into purging from sins, by which the speaker achieves his integrity (v. 14*b*).

Perhaps the primary contribution that Psalm 19 offers to this cluster of psalms is both cosmic and personal. Set beside the cosmos, *tôrâ* is the earthly repository of God's glory. At the same time, Psalm 19 internalizes the life of piety: the king's battlefield becomes inscribed on the landscape of the speaker's heart. In the struggle for moral integrity, enemies become iniquities (19:13-14) to be replaced ultimately by God's "goodness" and "benevolence" (23:6) by means of *tôrâ*. As the ultimate object of desire, *tôrâ* points to the celestial portal that extends, perhaps even replaces, the earthly temple and provides a model of personal piety that takes the place of royal prowess on the battlefield.

In the entrance liturgies, moral qualifications are stipulated for admission into God's sanctuary. Psalm 23 concludes with the speaker's goal to dwell forever in the "house of YHWH" (v. 6). Having followed YHWH's "statutes" and "ordinances," the king lifts up his righteousness as warrant for victory (18:22-25) and for entrance into a "broad place" and "refuge" (18:20, 31*b*). Set beside Psalm 19, all these references—from precept to place—point ultimately to *tôrâ* as the refuge and the way, the "tent" and the "path." Psalm 19 establishes both the goal of the reader's ascent within the collection and the entry point of the community into life before God. As the community bears witness to the King of glory at his entrance into the temple (24:8-10), so all of creation bears witness to the God of glory at the breaking of the dawn. All in all, Psalm 19 provides the highest possible yet most personal vantage point for witnessing, indeed bearing, God's effulgent presence.[20]

CHAPTER 6

PSALMS AS CORPUS

W e have so far approached the Psalms from a variety of contexts, examining them for their poetic subtleties and generic distinctions, as well as discerning how they fit and function in various groupings and collections. As we proceeded, we broadened the range of our focus, from the single poetic line to the individual psalm to the cluster or collection. Now we enter the broadest and perhaps most difficult of purviews: the Psalms as a whole. To do so we must shift our focus from the *Sitz im Leben* of a psalm to its *Sitz im Buch,* namely, its placement and function within the book of Psalms. By casting our literary net wider, we also increase the range of interpretive possibilities. The psalmic whole, we shall find, is greater than the sum of its parts.

The Davidic "Torah"

The Psalter, as its editors arranged it, is a divided whole, a book of "books." As various collections and groupings were arranged and put into place, the Psalms came to be divided overall into five "books," each one concluding with a doxology:

> Blessed is YHWH, Israel's God,
> from everlasting to everlasting!
> Amen and Amen. (41:13 [Heb 41:14])

> Blessed is YHWH, Israel's God,
> who alone does marvelous things!
> Blessed is his glorious name forever!
> His glory fills all the earth!
> Amen and Amen. (72:18-20*a*)

> Blessed is YHWH forever!
> Amen and Amen. (89:52 [Heb 89:53])

> Blessed is YHWH, Israel's God,
> from everlasting to everlasting!
> Let all the people say, "Amen!"
> Praise YHWH! (106:48)

These doxologies stand apart from the particular psalms to which they are attached. The word "amen" in the Psalter, for example, is found only in the doxologies. The addition of these doxological endings yields the following structural division:

Book I: Psalms 1–41
Book II: Psalms 42–72
Book III: Psalms 73–89
Book IV: Psalms 90–106
Book V: Psalms 107–150

According to rabbinic tradition, the Psalter's fivefold structure finds its precedence in the Pentateuch, the Torah of Moses, as noted in the *Midrash Tehellim*: "As Moses gave five books of laws to Israel, so David gave five books of Psalms to Israel."[1] The statement claims David as the source of the entire Psalter. By the first century B.C.E., the Psalter was, in fact, attributed to David. Internally, the Hebrew Psalter, as we have noted, attributes nearly half the psalms to David. Other versions attribute even more. The Septuagint, for example, ascribes fourteen additional psalms to David. The Psalms scroll from Qumran Cave 11 describes David as having composed a total of 4,050 psalms and songs, which "he composed through prophecy given to him from before the Most High."[2] The tendency to attribute additional psalms to David inevitably led to the supposition that David was the author of the entire Psalter. As the first five books of the Bible came to be attributed to Moses, the Psalter became, in turn, the "Davidic Torah," or at least David's counterpart to the Mosaic Torah. Either way, given their common fivefold structure, the Pentateuch and the Psalter form the two poles of ancient Israel's faith: the word and deed of God, on the one hand, and Israel's response in prayer and praise, on the other.

The Ties that Bind

Such is one view of the Psalter's coherence, one that appeals to external grounds within the development of interpretive tradition: Davidic attribution and the Psalter's "pentateuchal" form. However, if one goes searching for coherence from *within* the Psalter, certain editorial and thematic features call attention to themselves. There is, for example, a discernible (albeit disjointed) movement from complaint-petitions to hymns. In Book I, for example, a string of complaint-petitions in Psalms 3–13 is broken only by one hymn (Ps 8), whereas the last five psalms of Book V burst forth with uninterrupted praise. The Psalter, moreover, begins by commending individual "meditation" on God's *tôrâ* or teaching (Ps 1) and concludes with a corporate call to all-encompassing praise (Ps 150).[3] Such overarching aspects, among others to be noted in this chapter, tie this vast collection into something of a single corpus.

One can also read the book of Psalms from a narrative standpoint. As is often noted, Books I–III (Pss 1–89) reflect thematic and editorial features that set them apart from Books IV–V (Pss 90–150). Interpreters have observed that Psalms 2–89 reflect a primarily Davidic or earthly view of kingship. Gerald Wilson has noted the strategic placement of "royal psalms" at the "seams" of the first three books (Pss 2, 72, and 89) and their striking absence in the transition from Book IV to Book V.[4] This movement is also paralleled, to some degree, with the decreasing number of psalms attributed to David (95 percent in Book I; 32 percent in Book V).[5] Taking their cues from Psalm 2, some interpreters refer to Books I–III as the "messianic collection" and Books IV–V as the "theocratic collection," which develops the theme of divine kingship over all creation.[6]

The pivot of the thematic shift from earthly to divine kingship is found at the end of Book III, specifically in Psalm 89, which recounts God's "eternal" covenant to David and David's dynasty in verses 1-37 (cf. 2 Sam 7). But in an abrupt about-face, the latter half of the psalm delivers a blistering protest against God's abandonment of the earthly monarchy (vv. 38-51). The covenant, the psalm attests, has utterly failed. By documenting its demise, Psalm 89 paves the way for subsequent psalms to laud God's exclusive kingship over Israel, the nations, and the cosmos. Psalm 90 marks the shift not only with its attribution to Moses (as opposed to David) but also by, on the one hand, focusing resolutely on the "power of [God's] wrath" (v. 11) and the eternity of God's reign (vv. 1-2) and, on the other hand, by lamenting the fragile finitude of human existence (vv. 3-10). This psalm, along with the remaining sixteen psalms that constitute Book IV, has been called the "answer" to the failure of God's covenant with David and the "editorial center" of the Psalter's final form.[7] Psalm 106 concludes Book IV with a plea for Israel's deliverance from exile (v. 47), to which Book V's opening, Psalm 107, responds with the testimony of former exiles gathered from all directions (vv. 1-3).[8] The Davidic psalms that sparsely populate Book V profile David as the king who "bows to the kingship of YHWH."[9]

Such a reading of the Psalter, with many details to fill in, suggests a narrative approach to the book that begins with the Davidic monarchy and ends with the exiles' return. It is a story that, as Nancy deClaissé-Walford argues, gives shape to Israel's identity, making possible its very survival in a postexilic age without a king and court.[10] Or as Steven Parrish contends, it is a story of "emergence" (Psalms 1 and 2), "establishment" (Books I–II), "collapse" (Book III), and "reemergence" (Books IV–V).[11] Such an approach works as far as it goes. No narrative schema, of course, can accommodate the Psalter in all its complexity.[12] But then *any* approach to reading the Psalms as a book is bound to lift up certain elements and neglect others.

Reading the Psalms as a Book

I propose an alternative but not unrelated approach to reading the Psalms *qua liber*. It is a reading that seriously considers how the Psalter begins, namely with Psalms 1 and 2, and traces the themes featured in these introductory psalms throughout the entire corpus. Without superscriptions, these two psalms provide the "hermeneutical spectacles,"[13] a right lens and a left lens, one could say, by which to read the Psalter from beginning to end. Psalms 1 and 2, in other words, serve to orient the reader to the Psalms by focusing on various thematic dynamics present throughout the Psalter. Another feature, one that is more rhetorically than thematically based, is the prominence of speaking voices in the Psalms. Reading the Psalms together establishes an intimate bond between speaker and reader: it compels the reader to take up the subject position of the speaker in some psalms and the position of the addressee in others. The outcome? That is for the reader to judge. As for this reader, the following offers my own reflections on the thematic and rhetorical dynamics that characterize the Psalter as a whole.

And so we begin at the beginning, the opening "chapter" of the Psalter.

Psalm 1

> How happy is the one who
>> neither walks in the advice of the wicked,
>>> nor stands in the path of sinners,
>>>> nor sits in the assembly of scoffers;
> But instead finds delight in YHWH's *tôrâ*,
>> meditating on his *tôrâ* day and night.
> That person is like a tree transplanted by channels of water,
>> yielding its fruit in due season,
>>> and whose leaves do not wither.
> Everything that person does will prove efficacious.
> Not so with the wicked:
>> they are, rather, like chaff,
>>> which the wind drives away.
> How fitting that the wicked
>> have no standing in the court of justice,[14]
>>> nor sinners in the assembly of the righteous.
> Surely,[15] YHWH knows the way of the righteous,
>> but the way of the wicked will perish.

This psalm features two contrasting characters, the wicked and the righteous. Both are vividly described, metaphorically and ethically.

The righteous one is like a flourishing, well-rooted tree; the wicked are like chaff blown away by the wind. The righteous one "meditates" on divine instruction (*tôrâ*), whereas the wicked do not measure up to ethical or legal standards.

As the source of delight and direction for the righteous, *tôrâ* is a central theme in the psalm. But a question of clarification needs to be posed: what is *tôrâ* in Psalm 1? It is commonly assumed that the reference designates the Psalter, that Psalm 1 has effected "a strange transformation" by which "Israel's words of response to her God have now become the Word of God to Israel."[16] Such a view, tempting as it may be, does not do justice to the standard notion of *tôrâ* as authoritative, divinely wrought guidance. The simple fact that the Psalter is composed primarily of human words directed to God in prayer and in praise (and, less often, to a human audience) counts against seeing the Psalter itself as *tôrâ*. How primarily human words directed to God in lament, for example, become "the divine word itself" remains unclear, at least within the Psalter's scope, for the Psalter makes clear that *tôrâ* is divine instruction.[17]

Nevertheless, Psalm 1 does have within its orienting scope a sense of the Psalter *in toto,* or at least a major portion of it.[18] But the Psalter is designated in Psalm 1 not by *tôrâ* but, as we have seen, by its verbal complement, the poetic outcome of the psalmist's "meditation" or discursive reflection (v. 2*b*). The other *tôrâ* psalms, as well as a creation psalm, are instructive in this regard. The concluding verse of Psalm 19 marks the psalm in its entirety as a discursive product of the "mouth" and "heart" (v. 15). Analogously, Psalm 104 designates itself as an offering of discursive praise that, the speaker hopes, is acceptable to God (v. 34*a*). By extension, then, Psalm 1 views the Psalter as a series of reflective responses to YHWH's word, the discursive consequence of continual reflection on divine *tôrâ*. As the deliberative result (rather than object) of the psalmist's "meditation," the Psalter is a verbal offering to God.

What does Psalm 1 do, then, for the reader of Psalms? First, this prefatory psalm instills a desire for righteousness. Second, the psalm sets the reader on a quest for YHWH's *tôrâ*, the source of delight and instruction for righteousness. But at the outset of this search, the reader is thrown headlong into a wholly different psalm, one that paints a vivid scene of conflict and strife.

Psalm 2

> Why do the nations rant,
>> and the peoples rave[19] in vain?
> Why do the kings of the earth take their stand,
>> and potentates conspire together,
>>> against YHWH and his anointed?
> "Let us tear off their fetters,
>> and let us fling off their cords from us!"
> The One who sits in the heavens laughs;
>> the Lord derides them.
> He then speaks to them in his wrath;
>> in his anger he terrifies them.
> "I hereby install my king
>> upon Zion, my holy mountain."
> I will tell of the decree YHWH has issued for me:
>> "My son you are; today I hereby beget you.
> Ask of me so that I will make the nations your heritage,
>> and your possession, the ends of the earth.
> You will smash them with a rod of iron;
>> like a potter's vessel you will dash them in pieces."
> So now, O kings, get wise!
>> Be instructed, O rulers of the earth!
> Serve YHWH with fear,
>> and rejoice with trembling.
> Kiss the son,[20] lest he become angry,
>> and you perish in the way.
>>> Indeed, his wrath is quickly kindled.
> How happy are all who take refuge in him.

Psalm 2 plunges the reader into the savage world of international conflict. The reader does not simply read about some conflict in the past; he or she must duck for cover! The composed judgment of Psalm 1 is replaced with shouting matches, rattling sabers, and derisive laughter. This "loud" and vivid picture of military conflict against Zion sets up what will prove to be a type-scene in the Psalter. But for now, the righteous individual and the wicked collectively described in Psalm 1 morph into YHWH's anointed king and the conspiring kings in Psalm 2. Neither psalm provides neutral territory; there is no middle ground. You are either on the side of the righteous, on the side of YHWH's chosen king, or you are against the God of *tôrâ*, the God of Zion.

115

Though widely divergent in content and style, these two psalms are bound together by at least two intertextual links. "Meditating" on *tôrâ* in 1:2 finds its counterpart and counterpoint in the nations ranting and raving in vain (2:1*b*): same verb, opposite meaning. This connection between the two psalms is cemented more positively by the opening word of Psalm 1 and the last colon in Psalm 2: "How happy [*'ašrê*]". Bound by beatitudes, Psalms 1 and 2 introduce to the Psalter two contexts for "happiness": refuge and righteousness—the security of divine protection on God's holy mountain, Zion, and the secure attainment of righteousness informed by God's *tôrâ*.

With the juxtaposition of two contrasting psalms, the hermeneutical sparks begin to fly, generated by their various consonances and contrasts. The conspiring nations are likened to pieces of a shattered pot; the wicked are compared to chaff blown away by the wind. The royal and the righteous are juxtaposed as paired symbols of strength derived from God. The *tôrâ* of Psalm 1, the source of delight and guidance, is consonant with the divine decree in Psalm 2 (vv. 6-9), which Zion's king declares with utter confidence, if not delight. Psalm 2 provides the first example of divine discourse, a source of vindication for God's anointed and of judgment against conspiring kings. Indeed, Psalm 2 concludes with a dire warning for these kings to wise up and serve YHWH, lest they "perish in the way," just like the wicked (vv. 10-12; 1:6). Such is the sum and substance of *tôrâ*.

Together, these two psalms introduce and interrelate various themes that, as we shall see, wend their way throughout the Psalter: righteousness and refuge, *tôrâ* and Zion, judgment and protection, justice and kingship, instruction and dominion, pathway and sanctuary, individual and king, happiness and wrath. Such paired themes find their precedence in the juxtaposition of these two opening psalms. They set the stage for the rest of the Psalter in which such themes interweave and evolve, together and apart. From the reader's point of view, Psalms 1 and 2, as "hermeneutical spectacles," train the eye and attune the ear to linger over these juxtapositions and themes and to discern how they are dynamically related throughout the Psalter's length and breadth. This is not to say that Psalms 1 and 2 can accommodate everything conveyed in the Psalter (as if any two psalms could). Rather, they serve as programmatic pieces designed to influence how one reads the Psalter selectively yet discerningly. Nevertheless, the reader's performance is never the same in any given reading of the Psalter. To put it another way, the conversations hosted among the psalms in the Psalter never unfold in quite the same way to the listener. The Psalter's dialogical fullness is never completed. In the mind of the attentive reader, it is ever ongoing.

Book I

Beginning with Psalm 3, complaint-petitions dominate the first "book" of the Psalter, with David's voice, as claimed by the superscriptions, reverberating throughout. Surrounded by enemies, the speaker professes trust in God's protection, a "shield" (3:1-3). YHWH responds, the speaker declares, "from his holy hill" (v. 4b; cf. 2:6). Who are these enemies in Psalm 3? They are "the wicked" (3:7; cf. 1:4-6). Who is the speaker? Psalms 1 and 2 bear on Psalm 3 by filling out the speaker's identity. Psalm 1 identifies the righteous person as the voice behind the petitions. Psalm 2 ensures that the voice is also royal. Psalm 3, thus, features a righteous king who is overwhelmed by his enemies and cries out to God in desperation. But whether associated with royalty or not, the figure of the righteous in Book I is often depicted as an object of oppression. In many psalms, the righteous find themselves attacked and persecuted by the wicked. Psalm 1, however, is exceptional: it gives no indication that the righteous are under assault. This opening psalm, instead, expresses serene confidence in the demise of the wicked (1:4-6). But as we find in Psalm 4, the righteous are also the distressed "faithful." Although they are "set apart" by YHWH (v. 3), they also find themselves in "dire straits" (v. 1). They, with David counted among them, utter these anguished pleas.

Although righteousness comes with trust (4:5), it also comes with poverty and deprivation. Book I significantly widens the profile of the righteous given in Psalm 1 by depicting the righteous as victims. "In arrogance the wicked persecute the poor" (10:2a). It is as if the wicked have taken an ax to the "transplanted" tree of Psalm 1! But God remains on the side of the righteous. YHWH is refuge for the poor (14:5), and it is for the poor that YHWH resolves to "rise up" and "place them in the safety for which they long" (12:6). "I have not seen the righteous forsaken or their children begging bread," claims the speaker (37:25). And yet, as another "Davidic" speaker admits, the righteous find themselves "poor and needy" (40:17). "YHWH's eyes are on the righteous, and his ears are open to their cry" (34:15). They have reason to cry out; they are "brokenhearted" and "crushed in spirit" (v. 18). "Many are the afflictions of the righteous," even as they are recipients of God's saving power (v. 19). The plaintive cry, "How long, YHWH?" (6:3; 13:1-2) matches the confident pronouncement of God's decree: "Today I hereby beget you" (2:7).

As for the wicked, they and the nations converge in Psalm 9; their demise is entirely of their own making, as they dig pits to fall into (vv. 15-17). Or they draw their weapons only to kill themselves (37:14-15). "Let them be caught in the schemes they have devised" is the plea intoned in 10:2b. Such is the destined "way" of the wicked (1:6). As "deliverance belongs to YHWH" (3:8), so also does judgment belong to the wicked. God "takes no delight in wickedness" (5:4) but "loves righteous deeds" (11:7).

In Book I, God is both king and judge. As king, God responds to pleas for deliverance (5:2). As the "King of glory," God takes up residence in the temple (24:7-10) and "sits enthroned over the flood" (29:10). The scope of divine kingship is widened even more in Psalm 33: as universal sovereign, YHWH is creator, and as creator, "all the earth" is commanded "to fear YHWH" (33:6-8). It is as king, thus, that YHWH will help "his anointed . . . with mighty victories" (20:6; cf. 2:6).

The other side of divine kingship is God's role as judge who calls the nations to account and condemns the wicked. But divine judgment also applies to the speaker, who welcomes it on account of his or her own "righteousness" (7:8). Echoing Psalm 1, Psalm 26 calls upon God to "prove" and "test" the speaker, who pronounces his or her distance from "evildoers" and the "wicked" (vv. 2-5; cf. 1:1): the speaker has not "sat with the worthless" nor "consorted with hypocrites" (v. 4; cf. 1:1). At the beginning and end of the psalm, the speaker insists that he or she has "walked in integrity" (vv. 1, 11). The speaker's greatest fear is being "swept away with sinners" (v. 9).

But are the righteous without sin? Twice in Book I, the speaker pleads that God not "rebuke" or "discipline" in anger (6:1; 38:1; cf. 39:13). The speaker in Psalm 25, moreover, pleads for God's mercy and benevolence to pardon his or her "great" guilt (vv. 6,

11). This righteous speaker is not without sin and affirms that YHWH "instructs sinners in the way" (v. 8). This penitential psalm blurs the sharply bifurcated world of Psalm 1, where the righteous do not "take the path that sinners tread" (v. 1). Sinners too, Psalm 25 insists, can be shown YHWH's "paths," God's "truth" (vv. 4-5). The righteous are beset by sin and punishment but are wise enough to confess and seek forgiveness (38:1-14, 17-19; cf. 40:11-12). "How happy is the one whose transgression is forgiven, whose sin is covered" (32:1).

Zion, refuge, holy hill: all take prominent places in Book I (e.g., 9:9; 11:1, 6; 14:6; 18:2; 15:1; 24:3; 31:3-4), as they also do in Psalm 2. Also prominent in both is *tôrâ*, the source of delight in Psalm 1. "I delight to do your will, O my God; your *tôrâ* is in my heart" (40:8). In Psalm 19, *tôrâ* is the source of life. "YHWH's *tôrâ* is perfect, reviving the soul.... YHWH's precepts are right, gladdening the heart" (vv. 7-8). Psalm 19 is vivid testimony to what one could call the "joy of *lex*," surrounded, not coincidentally, by psalms of *rex*. Psalms 18, 20–21 testify to the king's victory over his enemies, made possible by God. Psalm 18 features a vivid theophany (vv. 7-15) as testimony to YHWH's salvific power—power unleashed "from his temple" (v. 6b). Divine power, however, is occasioned by "righteousness"—not God's but the king's! In verses 20-24, the royal speaker lauds his self-righteousness as the motivating factor behind his deliverance by God. Here is where righteousness and victory fit hand in glove. Victory in Psalm 19, however, comes in the form of a life purged not of enemies but of iniquity (vv. 12-13).

Book II

Although many of the psalms in Book II are attributed to persons other than David, the earthly king still gets his due. In Psalm 61, petition is made to God to "prolong the life of the king" and that "he be enthroned forever before God" with "benevolence and faithfulness" appointed to "watch over him" (vv. 6-7; cf. 1:6a). In Psalm 45, a royal wedding song, the king is praised for his beauty and grace (v. 2), "glory and majesty" (v. 3), justice (v. 4), and military prowess (v. 5). But echoing Psalm 1, he is also praised for loving righteousness and hating wickedness (v. 7). So fulsome are such praises that the king is even addressed as "God" at one point (v. 6). Book II concludes with petition on behalf of the king's son that "he defend the cause of the poor" (72:4), that "righteousness flourish" (v. 7), that his dominion extend universally (v. 8), and that his fame last forever (v. 17). With this final psalm, "Of Solomon," earthly kingship is passed on to the next generation, accompanied by great expectations.

But for all the praise and petition the earthly king receives in Book II, the theme of divine sovereignty receives its due as well. Psalm 47, an enthronement psalm, praises YHWH as "a great king over all the earth" (v. 2*b*), "king of all the earth" (v. 7), and "king over the nations" (v. 8). David, or any Israelite king for that matter, is nowhere mentioned in this acclamation of God's sovereignty. Even more striking are the songs of Zion, clustered immediately after the royal wedding song. Psalm 46 proclaims God, "our refuge and strength," as the defender of the city while the "nations are in an uproar" (v. 6) and the "mountains tremble" (v. 3). God ends all wars and destroys all weapons (v. 9). Recalling the type-scene of the nations' conflict in Psalm 2, Psalm 48 paints a picture of international conspiracy against Zion, YHWH's "holy mountain" (vv. 1, 4-7). But instead of having a king empowered to defend the city (cf. 2:5-9), the mere *sight* of the city inspires panic and sends the invading armies fleeing (48:5-7). "In its citadels God / has shown himself to be a stronghold" (v. 3). God has established Zion forever (v. 8). Similarly, Psalm 65 praises the God of Zion for "silencing the roaring of the seas...the tumult of the peoples" (v. 7). Creation itself is God's kingdom. Or as the following psalms proclaim, "All the earth worships you" (66:4*a*); "Let all the peoples praise you" (67:3*b*, 5*b*);

> Let heaven and earth render praise to him,
> seas and everything that stirs in them.
> For God will rescue Zion
> and rebuild the cities of Judah. (69:34)

God's universal reign is self-sufficient. No king is required. Not just the father of a king (2:7), God is also the "father of orphans and protector of widows" (68:5). It is also God, "my King," who "will shatter the heads of his enemies" (vv. 21, 24; cf. 2:9).

As for the righteous in Book II, they remain "poor and needy" (70:5), afflicted with sins and foes (51:1-5). They thirst for God like deer in the desert thirst for streams (42:1). The wicked, however, "go astray from the womb" bearing "venom" (58:3-4). Their punishment will prompt the "righteous" to "rejoice" as they "bathe their feet in the blood of the wicked" (v. 10). The "God who judges on earth" ensures reward for the righteous (v. 11), who, according to Psalm 52, are well established, similar to the "transplanted" righteous in Psalm 1:

> But as for me, I am like a green olive tree
>   in God's house.
> I trust in God's benevolence
>   forever and ever. (52:8)

Divine victory over the nations and the establishment of Israel in the land are also given a botanical twist in the communal complaint of Psalm 44:

> You, by your own hand, dispossessed the nations,
>   but them you planted. (v. 2)

God plants the righteous individual in Psalm 1 and the nursery of a nation in Psalm 44. Both are victory gardens, yet gardens under threat. The first communal complaint in the Psalter, Psalm 44 complains to God, "my King," for having made Israel "like sheep for slaughter, scattering us among the nations" (vv. 11, 22). For this psalm, righteousness stems from a steadfast heart that holds up God's "covenant"—related to God's *tôrâ*—despite the odds (v. 17), absent a king.

As for *tôrâ*, God imparts solemn instruction in Psalm 50, summoning both heaven and earth in judgment against "his people" (v. 4). God declares total ownership of all animals, thus precluding any need to consume animal sacrifice (vv. 9-13). Instead of slaughter, God commands "a sacrifice of thanksgiving," one that acknowledges with gratitude God's power to save (vv. 14-15, 23). Hence, the challenge from the God of all creation: "Call on me in the day of trouble; I will deliver you, and you shall glorify me" (v. 15). While God's instruction takes on a distinctly priestly tone, in addition to the indictments against Israel for various "covenantal" infractions (vv. 16-20), the centerpiece of divine judgment is a call to rely upon God's saving power, the foundation for thanksgiving. Such is the psalmic *tôrâ* of Book II.

Book III

Book III opens with a query and concludes with a crisis. The speaker in Psalm 73 is so perplexed by the "prosperity of the wicked" that he or she confesses both envy "of the arrogant" and despair for having "kept [his or her] heart clean" (vv. 3, 13). When the speaker attempts to understand the problem, the task is too "wearisome" until a resolution is found in "the sanctuary of God" (vv. 16-17a). There, the speaker perceives the demise of the wicked (v. 17b). Instruction in theodicy is found in the temple, in a revelation of God's judgment. From Zion, another psalm proclaims, God "broke the flashing arrows, the shield, the sword, and the weapons of war" (76:3; cf. 46:9). Zion is a source not only of revelation but also of salvation and peace. The God of Zion "inspires fear in the kings of the earth" (76:12; cf. 2:10-12).

Book III ends, however, without resolution over a much more intractable matter: the demise of the Judean monarchy, whose cornerstone is the Davidic covenant (89:19-37). The first half of Psalm 89 is a culmination of Psalm 2. It is a formalized, regularized guarantee of what is promised by God in Psalm 2. The decree "You are my son; today I hereby beget you" (2:7) is matched in Psalm 89 with

> He will call out to me, "You are my Father,
> my God, and the Rock of my salvation!"
> Indeed, I will make him the firstborn,
> most high among the kings of the earth. (vv. 26-27)

But God, the speaker complains, has reneged on the promise, violating the covenant (vv. 38-39). Near the end of the psalm, a question is posed: "YHWH, where is your benevolence of old, which you swore to David by your faithfulness?" (v. 49). No answer is forthcoming, so the speaker concludes the psalm by taking on a voice from the distant past: David, the "anointed," calls upon God to remember the taunts and insults of his enemies (vv. 50-51).

Between the query and the crisis, the psalms of Book III proclaim God as "King from of old" (74:12) whose power to destroy the primordial agents of chaos ("dragons" and "Leviathan") and to establish the order of creation (vv. 13-17) is called upon to vanquish present enemies so that "the poor and needy may praise your name" (v. 21). As in Psalm 89, Psalm 74 concludes with an exhortation that God remember and not forget "how the impious scoff" and "the clamor of your foes" (v. 22-23).

God's response bursts forth in Psalm 75 (vv. 2-5, 10), another judgment with moral exhortation specifically addressing the wicked: "Do not lift up your horn!" (v. 4b). God's judgment is that the "horns of the wicked [be] cut off, but the horns of the righteous shall be exalted" (v. 10). Likewise, Psalm 81 features divine discourse, an admonition that recites Israel's release from Egyptian bondage and the prohibition against worshiping foreign gods (v. 9). But Israel remains recalcitrant, prompting God to lament, "O that my people would listen to me, that Israel would walk in my ways!" (v. 13).

As for the ways of *tôrâ,* something new unfolds. Divine instruction in Book III focuses on the "teaching" of "YHWH's glorious deeds, his might, and the wonders that he has done" (78:4). God's works in history, along with "his commandments," are to be passed from one generation to the next, so they will not be forgotten (v. 7). Or in the words of the previous psalm:

> I call to mind YHWH's deeds;
>> yes, I remember your wondrous deeds of old.
> I meditate on all your works,
>> and on your deeds I ponder. (77:11-12)

As the object of "meditation," God's wondrous deeds are folded into the *tôrâ* of Psalm 1. In recounting the works of God's goodness, Psalm 78 emphasizes Israel's ingratitude and recalcitrance, culminating in God's rejection of "the tent of Joseph" and God's choice of "Judah, Mount Zion, which he loves" (vv. 67-68). Along with Zion, God "chose his servant David," the only internal mention of David in Book III outside of Psalm 89. David was taken from "the nursing ewes...to be shepherd of his people Jacob" (v. 71). Psalm 78 is followed by two psalms that plead for mercy and for Jerusalem's restoration (79:1-7; 80:14-19). Tellingly, Psalm 80 addresses God as "Shepherd." Before Psalm 89, Book III already makes the shift from David, the shepherd boy turned king, to God, "Shepherd of Israel." The plant that God cultivated in the promised land in 44:2 is, in Psalm 80, the "vine" transplanted from Egypt but ravaged by a "boar" and burned by fire (vv. 8-13, 16). The type-scene of international conspiracy once again lifts its ugly head, but this time with various parties specifically named (83:2-8). The speaker pleads that God "make them...like chaff before the wind" (v. 13), just as the wicked are destined in Psalm 1. But Psalm 83, unlike Psalm 2, ends only in petition, without assurance from God and without a king for the people.

Another source of instruction is found in Psalm 86, whose

speaker is identified as "poor and needy" (v. 1) and describes God with a dense array of predicates and attributes. "Teach me your way, YHWH, that I may walk in your truth" is the speaker's request (v. 11). Such truth is, in fact, found in the way the speaker describes God as "good and forgiving, abounding in benevolence for all who call on you" (v. 5) and as incomparable "among the gods" (v. 8): "For you are great and do wondrous things; you alone are God" (v. 10). The height of instruction is found in verses 5, 15:

> But you are the Lord, God of compassion and grace,
>> slow to anger and abundant
>>> in benevolence and faithfulness. (86:15)

The pairing of benevolence and faithfulness is also found in 89:49, cast as a question in relation to God's promise sworn to David. But in Psalm 86, the chain of such central attributes is rooted in a much "older" tradition, at least from a narrative standpoint: God's theophany before Moses in Exod 34:6-7, which offers the most comprehensive and compact profile of God in all the Pentateuch, if not in all the Hebrew Bible.[21] It now finds its way into "David's" Psalter. In one brief petition to God, profound instruction is imparted that gets to the heart of God's "way" and "truth" in the world.

Instruction in God's ways in Psalm 86 is supplemented in Psalm 82, which lifts up God's justice over and against the gods. This Asaphite psalm takes the reader into the divine council as a hearing unfolds. God (*'ĕlōhîm*) issues an indictment against the gods (*'ĕlōhîm*): "How long will you rule unjustly and show partiality to the wicked?" (v. 2). God's charge against the gods is accompanied by the challenge to implement justice for the "weak and the orphan," "the lowly and the destitute" (v. 3). Justice for them requires deliverance "from the hand of the wicked" (v. 4). But the gods fail miserably at what is so essential to the divine way. God sentences them to death (vv. 6-7): the gods are destined for mortality. The psalm ends with the speaker's cry, an urgent petition that God "rise up" to "judge the earth" (v. 8), to take up and implement what the gods failed to do. God's justice, benevolence, and faithfulness: all are underscored in Book III, which lifts up God's sovereignty and justice above all other forms of sovereignty and justice (76:12), human or divine.

Book IV

Book IV, often considered the Psalter's editorial center, begins with a psalm of Moses (90) and concludes with a sweep of Israel's history (105–106), with nary a mention of David and the monarchy. Not so in between, however. Within Book IV lies a Davidic psalm that lives up to the promise of its pedigree. In Psalm 101, the speaking voice is deceptively royal. The psalm begins with the speaker's expressed intent to "study the way that is blameless" and the resolve to "walk with integrity of heart within my house" (v. 2), evoking intimations of *tôrâ* (cf. 1:2; 19:7, 13). The speaker's house, it turns out, is none other than a kingdom. The king signals his intent to "destroy" slanderers, indeed "all the wicked in the land" (vv. 5*a*, 8*a*), while treating favorably "the faithful in the land" (v. 6*a*). "Whoever walks in the way that is blameless shall minister to me," declares the king (v. 6*b*). This is not the talk of any ordinary head of household! In its own way, Psalm 101 represents the royal appropriation of *tôrâ* (cf. Deut 17:18-20). As a consequence, the king's prowess is no longer imperial, as one finds in Psalm 2. It is moral, albeit militantly so.

Elsewhere in Book IV, royal imagery is applied exclusively to God, as evinced in the robust, world-constructive language of the enthronement psalms (93, 95–99) where the acclamation resounds, "YHWH reigns!" (93:1; 96:10; 97:1; 99:1; cf. 95:3). God's kingship is universal and just (96:10). It is also bound up with God's role as creator:

> Let the heavens rejoice and the earth be glad;
> > let the sea and its fullness roar.
> Let the field exult and all that is in it;
> > then shall all the trees of the forest rejoice
> Before YHWH, for he is coming,
> > for he is coming to judge the earth.
> He will judge the world rightly,
> > and the peoples with his faithfulness.
> > > (96:11-13 [see also 98:4-9])

As "a great King above all gods," YHWH lays claim to all creation (95:3-5) and Israel's "victory" (i.e., survival) for all to see (98:1-3). The language of imperial destruction is muted. Rather than be silenced, the sea is commanded to roar (96:11*b*; cf. 65:7). All the earth is exhorted to "make a joyful noise before the King, YHWH"

(98:6*b*). Such is God's reign. These psalms redraw the picture of divine sovereignty captured in Psalm 2, of YHWH's greatness in Zion (99:2; 2:6), but without the "son," the Davidic king.

Set apart from these psalms, however, is Psalm 94, and its insertion within the enthronement cluster results in a generative juxtaposition, not unlike what one finds with Psalms 1 and 2. Here, YHWH is not called "King" but "Judge" (94:2). Instead of nations seething and conspiring, it is the wicked who are killing "the widow and the stranger" and murdering "the orphan" with impunity (vv. 6-7). After noting such atrocities, the speaker imparts a lesson about God's supreme ability to perceive and to chastise. "How happy are those whom you discipline, YHWH, and whom you teach from your *tôrâ*" (v. 12). "Justice will revert to righteousness, and all who are upright in heart will follow it" (v. 15). As for the wicked, God "will wipe them out" (v. 23). As with the Psalter's introduction, Psalm 94 and its royal neighbors sustain the interplay between *tôrâ* and kingship. But now, kingship has become primarily divine and *tôrâ* more militant, indeed, more royal. What is left for David is the resolve to "study the way" and to purge his household (Ps 101).

With a psalm of Moses as its opening, Book IV marks a significant shift away from the trappings of earthly royalty and to the primacy of God's glory. Before God's wrath, mortals are mere "grass"; they are "like a dream" (90:5; cf. 102:3-11). Yet protection is afforded them: God is deemed "our dwelling place" (90:1), "my refuge and my fortress" (91:2). God assumes the role of royal protector: "I will protect those who know my name" (v. 14). No other help is needed.

Book IV concludes with an expansive view of God's sovereign reign, one that extends to all creation and history. It begins with Psalm 102, a desperate prayer from one whose "days pass away like smoke" and are "like an evening shadow; I wither away like grass" (vv. 3, 11; cf. 90:5). With a prayer directed to the "enthroned" God, the speaker offers assurance that "YHWH will build up Zion" and "regard the prayer of the destitute" (v. 16*a*, 17) and envisions a time "when the peoples assemble together, and kingdoms to worship YHWH" (v. 22). The psalm concludes with the telling benediction:

> Let the children of your servants live securely,
>   and their offspring be established before you. (102:28)

Gone is the concern that David—YHWH's "servant"—and *his* children be established forever on the throne (cf. 89:28-37). Instead the concern is that *all* God's servants and their progeny "be established." David is democratized among the righteous.

Psalm 103 responds in thanksgiving while noting that "mortals" are like "grass" and the "flower of the field," easily blown away by the wind (vv. 15-16; cf. 1:4). However, to quote an earlier thanksgiving psalm:

> The righteous will sprout like the palm tree;
>> they will grow like the cedar in Lebanon.
> Those planted in YHWH's house
>> will flourish in the courts of our God.
> They will still bear fruit in old age;
>> lush and fresh they will be. (92:12-14)

This passage specifically recalls the arboreal image of Ps 1:3 (see also 52:8). Once planted by flowing channels, the righteous (now plural) flourish as majestic trees at a tender *old* age within the temple. The righteous have matured.

In Book IV, God remains a gardener, cultivating the righteous, as much as God remains "merciful and gracious, slow to anger and abundant in benevolence" (103:8; cf. 86:15). Parental imagery also pertains: "As a father has compassion for his children, so YHWH has compassion for those who fear him" (103:13). Sonship is extended to all who "keep his covenant and remember to do his commandments" (v. 18). God's heavenly dominion (v. 19) extends to creation (Ps 104) and history (Pss 105, 106), both of which show forth God's "wondrous works" (105:2; see 104:24). Both historical psalms marvel over YHWH's covenant with Israel, a covenant rooted not in David but in Abraham, Isaac, and Jacob. It is God's sworn promise of the land (105:8-11), a covenant of compassion that ensures Israel's survival amid exile (106:44-46). But Book IV concludes with one work of wonder that remains unfulfilled:

> Save us, YHWH our God!
>> Gather us from among the nations,
> to render thanks to your holy name
>> and to glory in your praise. (106:47)

Behind this final petition is God's expansive work in the world— God's international, indeed, cosmic dominion, as claimed throughout Book IV. Only a God who is enthroned above heaven and earth, whose benevolence is as high as the heavens are above the earth (103:11), is capable of bringing home those scattered "among the nations."

Book V

The last and, by far, largest "book" of the Psalter is a vast assortment of different psalms and themes, ranging from complaint-petitions to thanksgiving songs and hymns, from *tôrâ* to king, both human and divine. This final collection can be seen as a representative smorgasbord of many of the psalms that have come before. David is featured here with his own mini-collection (Pss 138–145), along with Solomon (Ps 127). And amid the great variety are found not a few generative juxtapositions.

As is well noted, the first psalm responds in kind to the question concluding the final psalm of Book IV:

> "Give thanks to YHWH, for he is good,
>   for his benevolence endures forever!"
> So say the redeemed of YHWH,
>   those he has redeemed from the hand of the enemy,
> those he has gathered from the lands,
>   from east and from west,
>   from north and from south. (107:1-3)

Indeed, Psalm 107 is thoroughly focused on God's gathering of the lost from various predicaments, whether from the desert or at sea, in prison or from illness. Princes, however, receive only contempt: they continue to "wander in trackless wastes" (v. 40).

But there is one prince who remains favored: David. Psalm 108 is a combination of two earlier Davidic psalms (each a *miktām*): Pss 57:6-11 and 60:4-12. The first part praises God for God's steadfast "benevolence" and "faithfulness" (108:4); the second part petitions for "victory" and complains of rejection by God (vv. 6, 11). "Grant us help from the foe, / human deliverance is worthless" (v. 12). But "with God we will triumph; / he will trample our foes" (v. 13). In this Davidic psalm, God is the victor. Psalm 110, however, recalls more forcefully God's power invested in the earthly king: "YHWH will extend your mighty scepter from Zion. Rule in the midst of your enemies!" (v. 2). The psalm even recalls the divine decree of Psalm 2:

Your people stand willing and ready,
    on the day of your strength.
"In holy splendor, go forth out of the womb,
    before the dawn!
        Like the dew, I have begotten you."[22] (110:3)

The intimate bond between God and king is, once again, framed in the language of sonship. Indeed, more vivid than Psalm 2 are the veiled references to the king's birth in Psalm 110. Even more surprising, however, is the following verse:

YHWH has sworn an oath and will not revoke (it):
    "You are a priest in perpetuity by virtue of Melchizedek."
                                                    (v. 4)

One might assume from reading just the first colon that the "oath" given to the king and backed by God's word is the preservation of the Davidic dynasty (e.g., 89:28; cf. 132:11-12). Not so: David is invested with priestly identity, rooted in Abrahamic tradition (see Gen 14:17-20). He is the recipient of a priestly, rather than royal, promise from God, even as he is assured of victory over his enemies in battle (vv. 5-6; cf. 2:9).

Psalm 132 also provides a twist on David's royal persona. It beseeches God to remember how the David of long ago searched diligently for a suitable "resting place" for YHWH (vv. 1-10). David's hardship is suffered on behalf of Zion's founding. Call it the passion of the king. His painful mission is encapsulated by his own oath (vv. 3-5), to which YHWH responds in kind:

YHWH has sworn to David a true oath,
    which he will not revoke:
"One from the fruit of your loins
    I will set on your throne.
If your sons keep my covenant,
    and my precepts that I shall teach them,
then their sons, too,
    shall sit on your throne forevermore." (132:11-12)

In contrast to Psalm 89, the Davidic covenant in Psalm 132 has turned conditional (cf. 89:3-4, 28-37; 2 Sam 7:12-16). The continuance of the dynasty now rests solely on the king's obedience to YHWH's covenant (cf. Ps 89:30-31; 2 Sam 7:14*b*). The kingdom, thus, has ceded its precedence to God's *tôrâ*. Even if it falls (and it did), there remains *tôrâ* (cf. Isa 40:6-8).

Finally, Psalm 118, a royal thanksgiving psalm, resembles Psalm 18. Verses 10-12, in particular, portray the speaker surrounded by "all nations," which are "cut off" by him "in the name of YHWH." "Songs of victory" are played "in the tents of the righteous" (v. 15), and the speaker commands that "the gates of righteousness" be open, through which "the righteous shall enter" (vv. 19-20). Through it all, the king acknowledges God's power in bringing about victory, a royal victory.

It is no coincidence, however, that this final royal psalm is set next to the largest psalm of the Psalter, the "Psalm of the Law," and for good reason. All 176 verses of Psalm 119 are devoted to explicating the speaker's love for and dedication to *tôrâ*. In *tôrâ*, true righteousness is found:

> You have ordained your righteous decrees;
>   they are most trustworthy. (v. 138)

> Your righteousness is an everlasting righteousness;
>   your law is true. (v. 142)

> The righteousness of your decrees endures forever.
>   Give me understanding so I will live! (v. 144)

Consonant with Psalm 1, the speaker "meditates" on *tôrâ*, the source of delight and guidance, the object of the speaker's love:

> I rejoice in the way of your decrees
>   as in all riches.
> I will ponder your precepts,
>   and look upon your pathways. (vv. 14-15)

> I am consumed with longing
>   for your judgments every moment. (v. 20)

> Let me understand the way of your precepts,
>   so that I may ponder your wondrous works. (v. 27)

> Direct me on the path of your commandments,
>   for in it I find delight. (v. 35)

> I find my delight in your commandments,
>   which I love.
> My hands I lift up to your commandments, which I love,
>   and I will ponder your statutes. (vv. 47-48)

Had not your *tôrâ* been my delight,
    I would have died in my misery. (v. 92)

Nowhere else in the Psalter is *tôrâ* deemed the object of "love." Torah piety has reached its mystical height in Psalm 119. YHWH's *tôrâ* is construed as cosmically transcendent—"firmly fixed in heaven" as much as the earth is firmly "established" in YHWH's faithfulness (vv. 89-90).

At the Psalter's beginning and now in its final "book," *tôrâ* and kingship remain tightly juxtaposed. And in the latter case, the positions are strategically reversed. The "Psalm of the Law" in effect overwhelms the psalm of royal victory. Victory may be for the righteous, as Psalm 118 attests (vv. 15, 19-20), but it is found in *tôrâ*. Indeed, to walk with integrity, "in YHWH's *tôrâ*" (119:1), is itself a victory, one of right desire over sin (vv. 133, 139, 176) and over the wicked (see vv. 78, 84-88, 98, 110, 122, 134, 150-51, 157). "How can a young man keep his pathway pure? / By keeping it according to your word" (v. 9). The royal figure of psalms past has become the diligent follower of *tôrâ*:

Even though princes sit scheming against me,
    your servant ponders your statutes.
Yes, your decrees are my delight,
    they are my counselors. (vv. 23-24 [see also v. 161])

The lover of law carries an air of royalty (see also v. 46). Moreover, Psalm 119 has taken up all that has come before in the Psalter, from complaint to praise, and filtered it through the lens of *tôrâ*.

A comparable juxtaposition is found between Psalm 110, discussed above, and the following "twin" psalms 111 and 112, which render profiles of the righteous—both God's and the individual's. Psalm 111 praises God's "righteousness" (v. 3), whose "works" are "studied ($\sqrt{}$ *drš*) by all who delight in them" (v. 2). The psalm pairs together "the works of his hands" and YHWH's "precepts": both are estimable and reliable (v. 7). While the "works" of God are "studied," God's precepts are to be performed and practiced (vv. 8, 10*b*), and the result is a "good understanding" (v. 10*b*). "The fear of YHWH is the beginning of wisdom," so the psalm concludes in praise (cf. Prov 1:7). What Psalm 111 does for God, Psalm 112 does for the individual who "fears YHWH" and "delights exceedingly in [YHWH's] commandments" (v. 1). Like God, the individual is "gracious, merciful, and righteous" (v. 4*b*; see 111:4*b*). Righteousness endures for both God and individual (111:3; 112:3, 9). These "twin" psalms offset or, better, reset the militant royalty of Psalm 110. If the king profiled in Psalm 110 becomes the voice of Psalm 111—the voice of gratitude—then royalty changes into laity! The king becomes a sage and is counted among the righteous in Psalm 112.

Similarly, the royal "passion" of Psalm 132 is balanced by the calming demeanor of Psalm 131, on the one hand, and the celebration of community in Psalm 133, on the other. The speaking voice of Psalm 131 refrains from being caught up in the wonder of God's great works and instead commends a life of contentment, as embodied by a child with its mother. At the other end, Psalm 133 celebrates the blessing of familial unity, likened to "oil on the head," dripping "upon the beard" (133:2), and to the dew that falls on Zion (v. 3). Although Psalm 132 concludes with God's commitment to David and his house (vv. 17-18), it is Zion, God's residence, that is developed in the subsequent psalms (134–135), offsetting the promise made to David.

Psalm 145 has been called the "climax" of the Psalter, for it is the final psalm that immediately precedes the concluding Hallelujah psalms. Thematically, the psalm addresses God as "King" (v. 1) and pronounces a portion of YHWH's confession (v. 8), coupled with testimony of universal compassion (v. 9). The speaker pronounces his resolve to "meditate on [YHWH's] wondrous works" (v. 5). YHWH's "deeds" match YHWH's "words" in faithfulness (v. 13*b*). "Righteous is YHWH in all his ways, / and loving in all his deeds" (v. 17). And recalling the final verse of Psalm 1: "YHWH protects all who love him, / but all the wicked he destroys" (v. 20). Psalm 145 is thematically a summary psalm. But it does not mark the Psalter's formal conclusion. That is reserved for the final series of psalms, all five of them. Psalm 146 admonishes listeners:

> Put no trust in princes,
>> or in mortals, in whom there is no salvation.
> Their breath departs, and they return to the ground;
>> on that day their plans perish. (vv. 3-4)

All kings, Davidic or otherwise, are mortal, and their plans and promises die with them. The only one worthy of trust is God, "who made heaven and earth, the sea, and all that is in them," the one who "renders justice for the oppressed; / who gives food to the famished" (vv. 6-7), who "protects immigrants, / ... sustains the orphan and the widow, but makes crooked the way of the wicked" (v. 9; cf. 1:6). As the object of God's care, the righteous one of Psalm 1 is identified with the most vulnerable in society.

Celebrating God's majesty and power with exquisite praise, Psalm 147 acknowledges the gathering of the vulnerable ("outcasts") and the rebuilding of Jerusalem (v. 2). It concludes with testimony to the wide-ranging efficacy of God's "word," which sustains creation and constitutes Israel's ethos (vv. 15-20). Psalm 148, in response, calls upon all creation, from angels to sea monsters to the "kings of the earth," to render praise. But, according to Psalm 149, there are kings who refuse to do so and, thus, deserve to be bound "with fetters" (v. 8). Psalm 149 provides a fitting conclusion to Psalm 2, but with a twist. It is not the king but God's people who are "to execute vengeance on the nations and punishment on the peoples" (v. 7). Ultimately, however, such conflict is left aside as the Psalter reaches its conclusion in universal praise: "Let everything that has breath praise YHWH!" (150:6). Not only are the exiles gathered to become a reconstituted people; all creation joins together in praise to God. And the reader, once having taken up David's voice of complaint and thanksgiving, has now become the worship leader of the cosmos.

CHAPTER 7

PSALMS AS THEOLOGICAL ANTHROPOLOGY

God behaves in the psalms in ways he is not allowed to
behave in systematic theology.
　　　　　　　　—Benedictine Sebastian Moore[1]

With the Psalter in all its variety and coherence in view, the opportunity now presents itself to explore a sampling of theological accents conveyed in the Psalms. Common to all the various genres and collections that constitute the Psalter is their primary object of discourse, God, who is as irreducibly complex as the Psalms are literarily diverse. In the Psalms, the God who commands is also the God who sustains. The God of royal pedigree and the God of the "poor and needy," the God of judgment and the God of mercy, God's hidden face and God's beaming countenance: all are well represented in the Psalter. In the Psalms, the personal, kinship theology of the individual petition meets the cosmic, kingship theology of the enthronement psalm. It is no wonder, then, that Martin Luther regarded the Psalms as the "little Bible" (*die kleine Biblia*).[2] Given its rich diversity in form and content, the Psalter is Scripture's most integrated corpus. On

David's many-stringed lyre, as it were, can be heard almost every theological chord that resounds throughout the Hebrew Scriptures, from covenant and history to creation and wisdom.[3]

The complexity of this vast corpus, however, has not dissuaded interpreters from discerning a theological center or framework for the Psalter. A recent proposal is "refuge," a psalmic motif that points toward God's sovereign reign.[4] But, as with any proposal for a single center, much of the theological substance of the Psalter is left unaddressed. Another proposal posits the dual focus of "refuge" and "pathway," which recognizes God not only as sovereign and savior but also as lawgiver and guide.[5] One can, of course, identify additional theological accents, as we shall see.

In addition to its multifaceted focus on God, the Psalter provides an equally thick description of the human self, endowed with glory and honor yet afflicted with finitude and suffering. The Psalter presents a profile of the human self that plumbs the anguished depths of the soul while scaling the heights of human integrity and power. Psalmic poetry, in short, is as revealing about the human condition as it is about God. Indeed, God and the human self are bound together in the Psalter, as Psalm 8 vividly points out.

> When I gaze upon your heavens, the works of your fingers—
>   the moon and the stars that you have established—
> "What are human beings that you call them to mind,
>   mortals that you care for them?"
> You have made them slightly less than the divinities;[6]
>   with glory and honor you have crowned them. (8:3-5)

For the psalmist, the question of human identity cannot be posed without reference to God's identity as creator, and vice versa. Indeed, the question posed in Psalm 8 naturally leads to its converse: "Who *are you*, O LORD, that you call us to mind, that you care for us?" In this psalm, the question of human identity is raised in response to God's majesty in creation. The answer, however, comes as something of a surprise. Instead of lamenting the smallness of humanity amid the immensity of the universe (cf. 144:4), the psalmist rejoices in humanity's God-given glory and power, comparable to the claim in Genesis 1 that humanity was made in God's "image" (Gen 1:26-27).

But that is just one psalm. Difficulties abound in any attempt to discern theological and anthropological coherence across the Psalms. In addition to its eclectic character, the Psalter's very medium—poetry—is by nature allusive and multivalent. The language of metaphor, so replete in the Psalms, resists conceptual uniformity. Complicating the task, also, are the differing levels of theological discourse evident among the Psalms. Certain psalms exhibit a greater degree of theological reflection than others— what could be called "second-order" reflection, in distinction from "first-order" discourse. "First-order" expressions about God and the human self can be found mostly among those psalms that convey a situational immediacy, such as the simple complaint-petition (e.g., 13). "Second-order" reflection, by contrast, has a home in more elaborate and mixed genres, such as the extended hymns of praise, songs of trust and thanksgiving, and psalms of instruction. Such psalms step back, as it were, from the immediate exigencies of life to render a more reflective, comprehensive profile of God and the human condition. But regardless of the kind of theological discourse they convey, the Psalms together facilitate a convergence of theological reflection and urgent existential concerns. The end result is a theological anthropology borne of faith that is borne of crisis and inquiry.

The Psalms, in short, offer a messy theology "from below." They consist primarily of human words that are either addressed to God or talk about God. The human voice, whether in complaint, praise, or instruction, is the primary vehicle of psalmic discourse. If the narrative material of the Bible recounts what God has done, and the prophetic and legal literature convey what God has said, the Psalms present, in turn, how the community responds to God's words and deeds. As a whole, the Psalms model the worshiping community's posture and conduct *coram deo,* and therein lies its prescriptive force. The fact that the Psalter, like the Torah, is divided into five "books" suggests that divine discourse and human speech, divine deed and human act—in short, divine and human "performance"—are bound together.

The following observations regarding the theological anthropology of the Psalms are structured around the various genres or patterns of discourse that constitute the Psalms, with attention also given to the Psalter's overarching shape. The basic genres provide vantage points for theological discernment. Each offers its own theological and anthropological perspective. Furthermore, as we have seen, the Psalter evinces a theological development that concludes climactically with hymns of praise (146–150). This overarching movement from petition to praise, from an anthropocentric to a theocentric orientation, is readily discernable, as noted earlier. The complaint-petitions have more to say about the plight of the human self; the hymns, in turn, focus resolutely on God and God's ways in the world. The final section of this treatment is devoted to the particular theological challenge posed by the imprecation psalms, the so-called "psalms of vengeance."

Complaint-Petition

The complaint-petition genre was not unique to Israel. Widely attested throughout Near Eastern antiquity, this genre, as with most genres, exhibits stereotypical language and structure such that it has more to say about the human condition than about the individual speaker's specific situation.

Human Self

Whether in the language of self-abasement, penitence, or righteous anger, the pray-er in these psalms speaks as one who is fundamentally in want (cf. 23:1). The psalmic self prays from a situation of need for deliverance and for God. Distress and deprivation set the condition for prayer. The complaint-petition psalms describe various forms of distress, from sickness and near death conditions (e.g., Pss 6:2; 38:1-7; 88; 102:3-5) to slander and persecution by unnamed enemies (e.g., 69:5; 71:13; 109). The pray-er depicts life in a world wracked by conflict, dis-ease, and death in all its manifestations: physical, social, and spiritual. The language of suffering, though vivid, is stereotypical. The enemies, for example, remain unnamed. Likened to ravaging "lions," the speaker's foes are the wicked who oppress the poor and are filled with pride (10:9; 17:2). They are "greedy for gain" (10:3) and act with impunity, claiming that God is oblivious to their malicious activity (94:7; cf. 64:5-6). When not surrounded by his or her detractors, the speaker complains of social isolation and loneliness (25:16), "a little owl of the waste places" or "a lonely bird on the housetop" (102:6b-7).

Of all the dangers that beset the psalmic speaker, death presents the ultimate threat and the condition of greatest deprivation.

Metaphorically described as the Pit, Sheol is the domain of the dead that lies beyond (literally "below") God's reign or presence (e.g., 88:4-6). Death is the abode that is devoid of remembrance, a domain "cut off" from God's intervening power ("hand"). In the "pit" of Sheol, praise is impossible.[7] Consonant with the metaphor, the psalmist refers to the death experience as a descent, or return, to the ground: "[W]e sink down to the dust; our bodies cling to the ground" (44:25; cf. Gen 3:19); "You turn humankind back to dust, and say, 'Turn back, you mortals'" (Ps 90:3). Equally vivid is the cry from the watery abyss:

> Save me, O God,
>> for the waters have reached my neck.
> I have sunk into deep mire,
>> without a foothold;
> I have entered the watery depths;
>> the flood has swept me up. (69:1-2)

To cry "out of the depths" (*de profundis*, 130:1) is to cry from the brink of death. For the the speaker, the threat of death is ever present, constricting and afflicting human livelihood and existence. Psalm 144, a royal lament, speaks of human existence as a "breath" and a "passing shadow" (v. 4; cf. 39:4-6; 102:11). Finitude and fragility indelibly mark the human condition: "I am a worm and not human, / an object of human disgrace and derision" (22:6). In the same breath, however, the speaker of Psalm 22 claims God "took [him or her] from the womb" and kept the speaker "safe on [his or her] mother's breast" (v. 9). But this God has now forsaken the speaker (v. 1). While relying utterly upon God, the speaker also calls God to account. This genre, more than any other, acknowledges the self's absolute dependence on God.

In a world torn by strife, honor (*kābōd*)—the social acknowledgment of God-given dignity—is invariably violated, and shame is the result (e.g., 44:15-16; 69:18-19). Frequent appeal is made to God to vindicate and restore one's honor.

> In you, YHWH, I take refuge;
>> let me never be put to shame;
>>> rescue me in your righteousness!"
>>> (31:1; cf. 25:2; 31:17; 44:15; 69:6-7)

The complaint-petitions aim at restoring not only a person's health and vigor, but also his or her honor or standing in the community (e.g., 26:1; 35:24; 43:1; 54:1).

The psalmist's felt dependence upon God is expressed in a near formula of self-identity in the complaints: "I am poor and needy" (e.g., 40:17; 70:5; 86:1; 109:22; cf. 74:21).[8] More than economic deprivation is implied. The psalmist acknowledges his or her essential neediness *before* God and *for* God. Most evocative are the images of the doe and "parched land" thirsting for God (42:1; 63:1; 143:6). Of all objects of desire, from righteousness to prosperity, God is acknowledged as supreme: "There is nothing on earth that I desire other than you" (73:25). Conversely, all "human help is worthless" (60:11).

As profiled in the complaints, the human condition is marked by distress, deprivation, and vulnerability. The psalmist is a wounded speaker. Hence, the pleas for help acknowledge an essential dependence on God. Self-sufficiency, indeed self-salvation, is a delusion harbored by those the speaker deems wicked. The urgent plea to God for help in situations of distress, moreover, constitutes an act of allegiance, a surrendering to divine control; for as often as the pray-er is identified as "poor and needy," he or she is also deemed God's "servant" (86:1-2; cf. 34:2, 5, 22; 69:17; 143:12).

But even in this role, the psalmist speaks from a position of power, a position of covenantal kinship that calls God to account for divine negligence or abuse. As an address to God, the complaint-petition affirms the self's active agency in asserting itself before God. And therein lies the paradox: the very act of appeal to divine agency from a state of abject dependence actually heightens the power of human agency. The human cry for help is itself a powerful affirmation of human dignity, violated yet destined for restoration. The cry of dereliction is not the cry of resignation or despair; it is the cry for vindication, the cry for justice. The bold language of the complaint, in short, rests on an intensely personal, trusting, and empowering relationship between God and the petitioner.

God

God's nature as profiled in the psalmist's complaint and prayer has little to do with abstract, self-defining attributes (e.g., immutability and eternity). Rather, the God to whom the speaker prays is considered personally and compassionately engaged. God is cast, first and foremost, in the role of witness.[9] If the psalmic complaint gives testimony to distress and deprivation, God actively takes on the role of witness to receive such testimony. Of course, not just any witness is God. God is no dispassionate observer. The Psalms vividly convey the ancient confessional formula that God is abounding in mercy, compassion, and benevolence (ḥesed).[10] Specific to the complaint-petition, God is deemed the (only) one who can fully satisfy and deliver. The complaints reflect a personal God who is accessible and even open to argumentation and rebuke: "Why are you so far from helping me?" (22:1b); "Why do you sleep, YHWH?" (44:23); "You have renounced the covenant with your servant" (89:39a). Such bold language serves to challenge and motivate God to respond to human distress: "In my distress I cry to YHWH, that he may answer me" (120:1).

As the singular object of petition, the God of Israel is deemed the supreme agent of salvation: "You are the God of my salvation; / for in you I hope all day long" (25:5). Salvation, or more broadly "help" (43:5; 70:5), takes on various forms: deliverance from danger (4:8; 31:20), refuge or protection from the wicked (5:11-12), safe haven from oppression (7:9; 14:6), healing from sickness (38:1-5, 21-22), vindication in the face of slander or false accusation (69:4-5; 109:31), enactment of justice (10:18; 94:14-15), forgiveness of sins (51:1-2; 130:4), strength in the face of adversity (28:7), blessing amid deprivation (3:8b), and breathing room amid dire straits (4:1; 118:5). Various metaphors for God, from the natural to the political, depict God's protective, saving power for the needy and the victimized: refuge (5:11; 7:1; 14:6), shield (3:3; 5:12; 7:9), stronghold (9:9), rock (28:1; 42:9), fortress (31:2), shelter (31:20), shade/shadow (57:1; 63:7), raptor/wings (57:1; 61:4), light (4:6; 27:1), healer (6:2; 41:4), king (5:2; 10:16; 44:4), judge (7:11; 9:8), and warrior (7:12-13).

The one in need and the One who saves, the human being and the deity, mark a fundamental metaphysical distinction.

> May those who love your salvation
> always say, "God is great!"
> *But* as for me, I am poor and needy;
> O God, hurry to me! (70:4b-5a)

As for me, I am poor and needy,
but the Lord has regard for me.
You are my help and my rescuer;
my God, do not delay! (40:17)

The contrast between God and the human self is cast grammatically by the disjunction ("but") and existentially in terms of agency and power. In the complaint-petitions, human helplessness is met by God's beneficent power. The distinctiveness of divinity is highlighted all the more by the deity's incomparable nature:

All my bones declare,
"YHWH, who is like you?
You rescue the poor
from those who overpower them,
the poor and needy from those
who plunder them." (35:10)

Here, God's incommensurability is matched by God's unwavering resolve to bring about salvation: the resolve to rescue the "poor and needy" (35:10), deliver the oppressed (13:7-9), and vindicate the righteous (71:20-21).

Despite the absolute distinction that divinity holds over humankind, the psalmist appeals to a quality of relationship without which prayer would not be possible, namely, God's responsive concern to human need. The speaker appeals to God's solidarity with the needy: "For he stands at the right hand of the needy, / to save their lives from those who would condemn them" (109:31; cf. 12:5-6*a*). God's power is exhibited in God's responsiveness to the cries of the needy. What makes possible reliance upon God, the psalmist affirms, is essential to God's relational character, most frequently captured by one word: *hesed,* or "benevolence" (NRSV "steadfast love"). Appeals are made to God to act salvifically "for the sake of" or "according to your *hesed*" (6:4; 25:7; 109:26). On the one hand, *hesed* is the divine impetus for "salvation" (85:7) and, on the other, the divine warrant for the psalmist's deliverance (13:5) and forgiveness (25:7). God is called upon to enact *hesed* as the basis for establishing refuge (17:7). *Hesed* finds in the Psalms its semantic partners in "faithfulness" (*'ēmet,* 25:10; 36:5; 86:10) and "compassion" (*raḥămîn,* 25:6). God's *hesed* is both binding and spontaneous, a mark of covenantal loyalty and a sign of God's heartfelt concern. The psalmist celebrates the value and vastness of God's *hesed* (57:10), which provides refuge and sustenance for "all people" (36:7-8). Far from being a fleeting emotion or spontaneous act of the will, God's *hesed* is grounded in and bound to the promise of divine initiative:

> Has [YHWH's] benevolence come to an end forever?
> Has his promises ceased for all time?
> Has God forgotten to be gracious?
> Has he closed up his compassion in anger? (77:8-9)

Hesed is commensurate with God's promised word and, thus, can be found reliable in times of crisis. As such, *hesed* constitutes the foundation of God's covenant (*bĕrît*) with David (89:28). In this royal context, *hesed* is something sworn by God for David's sake and for the sake of David's progeny and kingdom (v. 49). God's *hesed*, freely established, binds God in benevolence to a people. It sums up the character of God's fidelity to a people's well-being that is freely initiated in grace. As the complaint section of Psalm 89 indicates, for God *not* to act in accord with *hesed* puts God's integrity in jeopardy.

Nevertheless, the benevolent God is not simply an instrument of deliverance, at the disposal of human need. Preeminently powerful, God is also eminently righteous (7:9, 11, 17; 129:4). In light of the competing religious systems of the ancient Near East, the moral goodness of a deity was not a foregone conclusion. Whether Mesopotamian or Greek, the various pantheons of antiquity were populated by deities known for their fickleness, cleverness, and mischief, not to mention ineptitude. But as for Israel's God, righteousness was considered a *sine qua non* of divine character: "God is a righteous judge, / a God who bears his indignation daily" (7:11; see 5:4-6).

As many complaint-petitions attest, God is not always available to the psalmist's beck and call. It is no accident, then, that the petitions frequently open with a complaint or rebuke (10:1; 13:1). Most anguished is the opening cry of abandonment in Psalm 22. Other pleas lament God's wrath, rather than absence, as the cause of distress (e.g., 6:1-2; 38:1-2; 88:7, 16). The complaint-petitions do not hesitate to implicate God in the particular crises that beset the speaker and to accuse God of willful negligence and even breach of covenant (44:17; 89:39). Rhetorically, such language makes God accountable to the petitioner. Theologically, the complaints acknowledge that God is elusive and not always available to human request. This God cannot be manipulated. The complaints give no explanation for God's abstention. God's inexplicable absence from the psalmist's situation is met only by more strident cries of complaint, along with a greater resolve to wait for God's intervening presence. The laments, thus, are driven by the hope that God can be compelled to pay attention to human plight. Without such hope, the psalmist is without a prayer, and God is bereft of *ḥesed*.

Thanksgiving Psalms and Songs of Trust

Compared to the complaint-petitions, the thanksgiving psalms and songs of trust offer a different yet related theological vantage point. Instead of desperate pleas for help, the thanksgiving psalms and songs of trust provide concrete testimony to answered prayer and display unwavering confidence in God's care and power to deliver. God's responsive nearness and the restored state of the human self are the theological markers of the thanksgiving psalms. The songs of trust cultivate a posture of humble reliance on and gratitude for the God who is preeminently trustworthy.

Human Self

As in the complaint-petitions, human fragility and suffering are acknowledged in the thanksgiving psalms: "Out of my distress I called upon YHWH" (118:5a), followed, however, by a testimony of deliverance: "YHWH answered me and set me in a wide-open place" (v. 5b). Briefer yet is the testimony: "When I called, you answered me" (138:3; cf. Jonah 2:2). Most extensive is Psalm 107, which features a litany of various scenarios of distress out of which "they cried to YHWH": the plight of refugees in the desert (vv. 4-5), imprisonment (vv. 10-12), sickness (vv. 17-19), and perils on the sea (vv. 23-27). Each disaster is met with deliverance: God guides the refugees to an "inhabited town" (v. 7), releases the prisoners (vv. 14-17), heals mortal illness (v. 20), stills the storm (v. 29), and finds a haven for the endangered (v. 30). In each case, an expression of thanksgiving follows. Other reasons for thanksgiving include victory in battle (118:10-16), personal deliverance from enemies (18:3, 17; 92:10; 138:7), agricultural bounty (65:9-

13), punishment of the wicked (75:8), and national deliverance (124:7).

In the thanksgiving psalms, the supplicant's lamentable condition is no longer front and center. The language shifts decisively from the psalmist's plight to God's remedy. The transformation of the psalmist's condition gives way to the transformation of the psalmist's disposition, as indicated also in the songs of trust: "I fear no evil" (23:4); "Surely, goodness and mercy shall pursue me all the days of my life, and I shall dwell in YHWH's house my whole life long" (v. 6). No longer dogged by unnamed enemies, the psalmist is now "pursued" by God's blessing and favor. Desperation and fear give way to confidence, joy, and gratitude. The speaker's transformation is consistently ascribed to God's initiative:

> You have turned my wailing into dancing for me;
> you have removed my sackcloth,
> and girded me with joy,
> So that my heart will sing praises to you and not keep silent.
> YHWH, my God, I will give you thanks forever. (30:11-12)

In response to God's act of deliverance or restoration, the speaker dedicates himself or herself to lifelong praise.

Compared to God's salvific agency, human help proves consistently impotent: "Better to take refuge in YHWH / than to trust mortals" (118:8; cf. 52:7). Human status, whether high or low, is but a "breath" by comparison (v. 9; cf. 103:15-16). Critical of alternative forms of help, the testimony of divine aid is also invitational: "Taste and see how good YHWH is! / How happy is the one who takes refuge in him!" (34:8). In the very same psalm, the testimonial assertion of thanksgiving provides a teachable moment: "Come, children, and listen to me! / Let me teach you the fear of YHWH" (v. 11; see also 32:8). In the thanksgiving psalms, "fear" of God is next to gratitude.

God

In the thanksgiving psalms, the imperative of petition becomes an indicative; the plea turns into testimony. "Hear my words, YHWH!" (5:1) is replaced by "I love YHWH because he hears / the voice of my petitions" (116:1). Such psalms provide a reflective look back at God's saving intervention. God is identified as "You who answer

prayer" (65:2*a*). The issue addressed in the petition of whether God
will provide help is resolved through testimonial assertion in the
thanksgiving psalm (34:4, 17). Most confessional is the affirmation:
"Our help is in YHWH's name" (124:8); or "My help is from YHWH, /
maker of heaven and earth" (121:2). Psalm 136 covers both the cosmic and historical range of divine "help," beginning with the work
of creation (vv. 4-9) and sliding effortlessly into the events of Israel's
journey to the land (vv. 10-22). God both "rescues" from "our enemies" (v. 24) and provides "food for all flesh" (v. 25).

The testimony of divine help provides the basis for various
statements about God's nature or character: "Though YHWH is on
high, he sees the lowly" (138:6*a*). The God whose throne is established in heaven (103:13) proves supremely accommodating to
those in need. Indeed, God's compassion bears its own mark of
transcendence.

> For as the heavens are high above the earth,
>   so great is his benevolence to those who fear him;
> as far as the east is from the west,
>   so far has he distanced our sins from us. (103:11-12)

The language of divine transcendence is ascribed to God's expansive *hesed*. It is in God's transcendent, majestic nature to be
compassionate.

Elsewhere in the thanksgiving psalms, God's immanent presence takes the fore: "YHWH is near the brokenhearted, / and he
delivers the crushed in spirit" (34:18); "We give thanks to you, O
God, we give thanks, for your name is near; / your marvelous
deeds are declared" (75:1). In the psalms of trust, confidence in
God's agency attains the level of *status confessionis*: "Only [God] is
my rock and my salvation, / my stronghold; I will not at all be
shaken" (62:2). God is claimed as the exclusive object of human
reliance (vv. 1, 2, 5, 6-7).

The posture of thanksgiving acknowledges the qualities of
divine beneficence, as in Psalm 103, which contains elements of
both thanksgiving and praise (vv. 2-5). Whereas certain complaints attribute the psalmist's plight to God's wrath, the topic of
divine anger in Psalm 103 turns into a theological statement of
assurance:

> Compassionate and gracious is YHWH,
>   slow to anger and abundant in benevolence.

He will not always find fault,
  nor will he nurse his anger forever.
He has not dealt with us according to our sins,
  nor repaid us according to our wrongdoings.
  (103:8-10 [cf. Exod 34:6-7])

Although deeply felt by God, anger does not constitute a divine trait or disposition. At most, divine wrath is a temporary state. More enduring and thus reflective of God's nature is God's mercy or compassion, most poignantly depicted in parental imagery: "As a father is compassionate to his children, so YHWH is compassionate to those who fear him" (103:13). This parental God of compassion, the God of *hesed,* is the God who prompts the speaker's thanksgiving and blessing.

As a summary reason for thanksgiving, the psalmist lifts up God's "goodness": "Give thanks to YHWH, for he is good; for his *hesed* lasts forever" (107:1; cf. 118:1; 136:1). Parallel to *hesed,* "good" (*tôb*) covers the fullness and constancy of God's gracious outreach, embodied in acts of creation, salvation, and provision (136:1-26).

Didactic Psalms

This loose category of psalms covers various types determined more by content than by form. It includes the Torah psalms (1, 19, 119), the so-called wisdom psalms (e.g., 32, 34, 37, 49, 111–112), temple entrance liturgies (15, 24), and the historical psalms (78, 105–106, 135–136), as well as several unclassifiable psalms (50, 73, 82, 115, 133). United by a declarative and prescriptive tone, these psalms share the expressed purpose of imparting instruction about the ways of God and of human beings in the world.

Human Self

By addressing the community or individual with instruction, the didactic psalms assume that human beings are teachable (73:24; 90:12) and thus capable of leading lives of integrity. The temple entrance liturgies of Psalms 15 and 24, for example, offer a veritable taxonomy of moral conduct that ranges from righteousness (15:2) and purity (24:4) to fulfilling oaths (15:4*b*) and lending money without interest (v. 5*a*). Those who perform such actions "shall never be shaken," established as firmly as the temple itself (v. 5b; cf. 112:6). Like the sage, the psalmist counsels restraint in anger (37:8) and the "fear of YHWH" (112:1), "the beginning of wisdom" (111:10). Such "fear," or heightened reverence for God, includes "delight" in God's commandments or obedience (112:1b), care for the poor (v. 9a), generosity (v. 5), and courage against evil (v. 7), as well as the practice of justice (v. 5) and mercy (v. 4). A life filled with reverence for God is a life led in happiness (v. 1).[11] Such qualities mirror God's own character (see 111:4-5, 7). A life of integrity is, in other words, a life of *imitatio Dei*.

A defining metaphor of human integrity in the didactic psalms is "pathway," a motif also shared, not coincidentally, by the wisdom literature, particularly Proverbs. To be "blameless" is to "walk blamelessly" (15:2). Those who disobey God "wander from [God's] commandments" (119:21b). The path of the righteous is sharply distinguished from that of the wicked (1:1, 4-6). Whereas a destiny of doom is reserved for the wicked (e.g., 1:4-5; 37:15), one psalm in particular (a meditation on theodicy) enviously acknowledges "the prosperity of the wicked" (73:3; see also 37:7, 34). This unsettling discrepancy of the wicked "always at ease" (73:12) questions the legitimacy of leading a morally credible life (v. 13). But the psalmist's despair turns into confidence upon entering "the sanctuary of God" (v. 17). There he or she gains the certainty of the demise of the wicked and regains the conviction to lead a blameless life before God.

Perhaps the most evocative metaphor of the teachable self is the image of the tree in Psalm 1. The righteous one is "like a tree transplanted by channels of water, which yields its fruit in due season, and whose leaves do not wither" (1:3a). Rich in religious connotation, the tree in Psalm 1 designates the righteous human being (see also 52:8; 92:12-13), the one who takes "delight" in God's *tôrâ* (v. 2a). The one who abides by *tôrâ* is destined to flourish and remain secure and efficacious in all matter of conduct. The wicked, by contrast, are mere "chaff" blown hither and yon (v. 4).

In relation to the complaint-petitions, the didactic psalms teach that salvation is not simply a matter of being saved *from* calamity or sin but also a matter of being saved *for* God. Such psalms claim that human beings belong to God and thereby remain accountable to God in their obedience and conduct. The God of the exodus, the

God of freedom, is also the God who gives form to freedom by fitting freedom for service to God. In the didactic psalms, human beings are called to responsible participation in God's world.

God

From the vantage point of the didactic psalms, God is regarded as guide and teacher. "Graciously teach me your law" is the repeated request in Psalm 119 (v. 29*b*; see also vv. 27, 33, 35); "You guide me with your counsel" (73:24*a*). Consonant with God's pedagogical role is that of judge:

> [God] calls to the heavens above
> and to the earth to judge his people.
> . . . .
> The heavens declare his righteousness,
> for he is the God of justice. (50:4, 6)

As judge, God is the author of justice. Psalm 82 regards justice as the *sine qua non* of divinity. Within the heavenly council, Israel's God judges the other gods as slackers in implementing justice for the "lowly and the destitute" (v. 3). The verdict is swift: God sentences the other gods to death for their failure to rule justly (vv. 6-7). But God's justice does not necessarily involve direct intervention from on high. In an acrostic psalm, the demise of the wicked is cast as self-inflicted (37:14-15). Here, the wicked are caught in their own devices, with their weapons turned against them. As guarantor of the created order, God has established the world such that the exercise of wickedness ultimately becomes self-destructive (see also 7:12-16).

Related to God the pedagogue and judge is God the lawgiver. As an object of desire and source of delight (1:2; 19:10), the "*tôrâ* of YHWH" is the compendium of authoritative guidance necessary for the community's life and order. "Law" is a gift for the sake of human flourishing, not the property of any human being or community. The "law" is preeminently God's "law"; it is neither the prerogative of the king nor the product of the community. For the psalmist, rather, *tôrâ* is revelatory; it comes from God's very "mouth" (119:72), like royal decrees, and is established in perpetuity (vv. 153, 160). The Psalms, in fact, rarely make mention of *mediated* law (103:7). Unmediated *tôrâ* reveals the just, wise God. As the direct discourse of the creator, *tôrâ* also has a cosmic reach.

Psalm 19 relates *tôrâ* to the cosmic manifestation of divine glory, symbolized by the sun, to underline *tôrâ*'s efficacious power and integrity: God's *tôrâ* confers wisdom, joy, renewal, enlightenment, and purification (vv. 7-9, 12-13). *Tôrâ* is also a medium of salvation. Psalm 119 unites God's "word" (v. 114*b*) and God's "salvation" (vv. 81*a*, 166*a*) together as a common object of hope and subject of judgment (vv. 155, 165-66). The psalmist broadens the scope of the "law" such that it is no longer confined to its historical manifestation at a particular place (Sinai or Horeb) through the mediation of a human individual (Moses). Creation itself bears witness to the divine ordinances (Ps 19). "Forever does your word, YHWH, stand high in heaven" (119:89). In these psalms, *tôrâ* is transcendentally cosmic.

As complement to God's cosmic commandments is God's activity in history, which several psalms recount (78, 105, 106, 135, 136). Psalm 78 presents a sweeping narrative of God's mighty acts in order to "teach" the next generation of God's wonderful works (vv. 1-8). In all these psalms, the event of the exodus, complete with various plagues, is given primary attention, but also recounted are God's guidance in the wilderness and the gift of the land ("heritage"). As the commandments reveal God's righteousness, so God's acts in history indicate divine forbearance and compassion as well as judgment. Israel's persistent disobedience is matched by God's reluctance to disavow Israel. In the face of Israel's stubbornness, God exercises restraint and acts with compassion and forgiveness (78:38) while remaining sorely aggrieved (v. 40).

> Nevertheless [YHWH] saw their distress
>   when he heard their cry.
> And he remembered his covenant for their sake,
>   and relented according to his abundant benevolence.
>   (106:44-45)

Paramount in the psalmist's litany of mighty deeds are God's benevolence and forbearance. Both capture the heart of God's character.

Praise Psalms

As the hymns of praise mark the culmination of the Psalter as a whole (see Pss 146–150), they also offer the culmination of ancient

Israel's understanding of God and God's way in the world. As the thanksgiving and didactic psalms mark a further step in Israel's theological work, the extended hymns of praise provide the most panoramic view of God, humanity, and the world.

The Human Self

In the psalms of praise (and elsewhere), dependency and dignity mark the human condition. The language of self-abasement, however, as found in the complaints, is lacking entirely. In its place is a self-abandoning exuberance that focuses resolutely on God. These psalms profile the human as *Homo laudans,* the "praising human," and in praise the full identity of the human self is reached. Psalm 8, for example, stands out for its high view of humankind (v. 5), in contrast to Psalm 144, a royal lament (see v. 4). Psalm 115, a mixed psalm of proclamation and praise, espouses a similarly high view of humanity: "The heavens are YHWH's heavens, but the earth he has given to human beings" (v. 16).

The endowment of royal dignity to all human beings, as claimed in Psalm 8, hermeneutically opens up the various royal psalms in the Psalter for general, if not universal, appropriation. For example, the prescription of proper royal conduct in Psalm 72 is thereby not limited to individual kings but applies to every person. All are called upon to lead lives of justice. The intimate, empowering bond between a father and son that legitimizes the Israelite king's dominion in Ps 2:7 is now, through the universal claim of Psalm 8, the warrant for each and every human being.

While certain psalms highlight the dignity and wondrous capacities with which human beings are endowed, several psalms of praise, like the complaints, acknowledge humanity's utter dependence upon the divine. The "strength" that human beings enjoy and exercise comes entirely from God (46:1; 68:35; 81:1). All forms of sustenance and blessing have God as their source. Dependence upon God is, the praise psalms stress, a feature endemic not just of humankind but of all creation (104:27-28). Most evocative is the reference in Psalm 84 to God's abode as home for human beings and animals alike (vv. 1-4). God provides a home for swallows as well as for persons, a home that is also God's home, the locus of praise (see also 23:6; 68:4).

Dependence on God is nowhere lamented but everywhere celebrated in the praise psalms. Because dependence is a feature that pervades all creation, the capacity to praise the source of all life has universal scope. The range of praise in the Psalms is nothing short of cosmic: "All the earth worships you; they sing praises to you, sing praises to your name" (66:4). From babbling infants (8:2) to raging seas (69:34; 96:11; 98:7) and fruit trees (148:9), all creation is called upon to praise the creator. Even the formidable Leviathan is transformed into God's partner in play (104:26). In a similar vein, Psalm 148 provides a roll call of cosmic participants in praise. It begins with the citizens of heaven, including the celestial spheres (vv. 1-4), and descends to the denizens of the earth, beckoning "sea monsters," meteorological elements, the land, and "wild animals" to render praise (vv. 7-10). Finally, all human beings, regardless of social status, gender, and age, are inducted into the expanding chorus (vv. 11-12). The call for all creation to give praise, as issued by the speaker of Psalm 148, fulfills the call for human beings to exercise "dominion" over creation given in Psalm 8 (and in Gen 1:28). The proper exercise of human dominion over creation is to enable all creation to give full, unfettered praise to God.

But there is more: compared to Psalm 8, humanity's place in God's cosmic world of praise is decentered in Psalm 104 (cf. Job 38–42). In this extensive litany of God's creative acts, human beings are scarcely mentioned; they are distinguished from the lions only because they take the "day shift" in their work (vv. 20-23), while the lions have the night. Plants are available for both cattle and people; wine and bread, however, are designated specifically for human use and enjoyment (v. 14).

In praise that is universally performed, universal peace is the end result. The psalms of praise envision a world devoid of conflict (46:9-10) and set for cosmic harmony. Even the "kings of the earth," perhaps the most reluctant of all to render praise to God, cannot escape the expanding, "edgeless" circle of praise that proceeds to envelop the cosmos. The command "let everything that breathes praise YHWH" concludes the Psalter (150:6). Such cosmic praise is directed toward the God who created the world as a variegated whole, a world in which *Homo laudans* play a significant, but not exclusive, role in the performance of praise.

God

The language of praise reflects the context and purpose of worship. The rhetoric of praise is not so much the response to specific acts of salvation (as in the thanksgiving psalms); rather it demonstrates that God alone is worthy of worship. This God is supremely "exalted in the earth" (46:10), enthroned as sovereign of the universe (47:8-9), and "enthroned on the praises of Israel" (22:3). Praise has its own credo: "Great is God and greatly to be praised" (48:1; cf. 89:7; 95:3; 104:1), and the profile of God's greatness bears unmistakably royal contours (e.g., 95:3; 96:4). As king, God is sovereign of the cosmos who elicits and solicits praise from all the earth. Praise is not just a response; it is an imperative.

Praise of God also bears a polemical edge: by proclaiming God as exclusively worthy of worship and trust, true praise exposes the idiocy of idolatry. Concluding a litany of God's wondrous deeds in creation and history, Psalm 135 issues a stern warning about idols, the manufactured images of other deities (135:15-18; cf. 115:2-8). Idols are nothing compared to God's power. The same goes for kings and princes, indeed for all humans: "Praise YHWH!... Put no trust in princes, / or in mortals, in whom there is no salvation" (146:1, 3).

In comparison to the thanksgiving psalms, the praise psalms' references to God's activity are cast more as divine attributes than as historically specific actions.

> How happy are those whose help is the God of Jacob,
>   whose hope is in YHWH their God,
> the one who *creates* heaven and earth,
>   the sea, and all therein;
>   who *keeps* faith forever;
> who *renders* justice for the oppressed;
>   who *provides* bread to the hungry.
> YHWH *sets* the prisoners *free*;
>   YHWH *opens* the eyes of the blind.
> YHWH *raises up* those bowed down;
>   YHWH *loves* the righteous.
> YHWH *guards* the immigrants;
>   the orphan and the widow he *sustains*. (146:5-9b)

Each clause in the psalm that highlights God's work is signaled by a participle in Hebrew that could also be rendered as a substantive (e.g., "creator," "keeper," "provider," "sustainer"). In the genre of praise, God's creative activity is ongoing and continuous (e.g., 104:2-10, 13, 14; cf. 148:2-4, 11, 19). Discrete activities are cast as divine patterns of behavior or roles: creator, healer, judge, provider, delighter, lawgiver. Specific acts are generalized in the praise psalms as characteristic modes of divine conduct.

It is in the praise genre that God's incomparable status is particularly highlighted: "For I know that YHWH is great; / our Lord is greater than all gods" (135:5); "Who is like YHWH our God, / who sits enthroned on high?" (113:5). God's incomparability presupposes absolute freedom: "YHWH does whatever he pleases, / in the heavens and on the earth, / in the seas and all the depths" (135:6). This God is not bound, covenantally or otherwise, to anything. God's concern for creation arises out of sheer freedom and delight (104:31*b*).

The praise psalms come closest to articulating God's essence, whose hallmark is "glory" (*kābōd*). Psalm 29 focuses almost exclusively on this fundamental attribute:

> Give to YHWH, O deities;
>> give to YHWH *glory* and strength.
> Give to YHWH the *glory* due his name;
>> bow down to YHWH in holy splendor.
> YHWH's voice is over the waters;
>> the God of *glory* thunders,
>>> YHWH is over mighty waters.
>
> . . . .
>> And in his temple all proclaim, "*Glory!*" (29:1-3, 9*c*)

The psalm dramatically illustrates God's presence made manifest in the form of nature-disturbing, preternatural power. Attested both visually and audibly, God's "glory" is as much a matter of divine substance as it is a quality acknowledged about God, a property conferred upon the deity by the worshiping community ("give to," "say"; cf. 68:34*a*). Elsewhere, "glory" is described as a brilliant effulgence of overwhelming "majesty" and "splendor" (21:5; 45:3; cf. 104:1*b*-2*a*, 31), as well as "power" and "strength" (63:2; 96:7). As in Psalm 29, God's glorious manifestation is associated with the temple or tabernacle.[12] God's "glory" trumps all alternative forms of worship as idolatrous (97:6-7). Originating from "above the heavens" (8:1; 113:4), God's "glory" is destined to fill all the earth (72:19; 85:9; see also Isa 6:3*b*).

The theme of glory is strongly connected with the language of theophany, that is, the language of God's in-breaking, transforming presence. Divine presence, for example, triggers cosmic convulsions: "Tremble, O earth, at YHWH's presence" (114:7a; see also 68:7-10; 104:31-32). God's glory, moreover, renders impotent all forms of conflict, both human and cosmic (46:9; 76:3). Before God, no element of creation remains rebellious. In praise (as opposed to lament), cosmic resistance is either erased or transformed. Leviathan is now God's playmate (104:26), and "sea monsters" roar in praise (148:7; cf. 93:3; 96:11).

It is in praise that God's transcendence is most palpably felt. Psalm 68, for example, speaks of God as the "rider in the heavens" (v. 33; cf. v. 4), yet also as "father of orphans and defender of widows" (v. 5). God's greatness is ineffable or "unsearchable" (145:3), yet God's hand is "open" to "fulfill the desire of every creature" (145:16). In the praise psalms, God's transcendent power and providential immanence are held not in tension but in balanced correspondence.

Inscribing the whole world as united in praise, the praise psalms conclude the Psalter. The ravages of conflict and dis-ease so vividly conveyed in the complaint-petitions have faded away. In the Psalter's overall arrangement, complaint and petition make way for thanksgiving and praise, conflict gives way to peace, enemies are reconciled, and *shalom* reigns. For the psalmists, praise is the vehicle for imparting the vision of a reconciled, flourishing world.

Vengeance Psalms

Perhaps the greatest challenge theologically for contemporary readers of the Psalter is found in the "psalms of vengeance," or imprecation psalms, which are dominated by the avenging cry against enemies (e.g., 12, 44, 55, 58, 83, 109, 137). Perhaps the most well-known example is Psalm 137, which begins with the poignant lyric:

> By Babylon's rivers—
>> there we sat and wept
>>> when we remembered Zion. (v. 1)

Yet the psalm concludes with the anger-charged stanza:

> Remember, YHWH, the Edomites,
>> on the day of Jerusalem's fall,

how they cried, "Raze it, raze it
to its foundations!"
O daughter Babylon, you devastator!
Happy is one who repays you in kind
for what you have done to us!
Happy is the one who seizes and smashes
your infants against the rock! (vv. 7-9)

In their brutal honesty, these psalms of vengeance articulate intense feelings of anger and betrayal. For readers who have suffered injustice and abuse firsthand, such psalms provide not only an outlet for outrage but a way of naming the injustices. These most bitter laments do more than simply vent; they redirect (self-) destructive anger to God, transforming the lust for vengeance into a yearning for justice, with "human wrath" giving way to "praise" (76:10a). The psalmists do not typically ask for the means or the right to take matters into their own hands. Indeed, they speak from a condition of abject powerlessness. Rather, they invoke the One who is the source of all power and justice by placing their petition squarely upon God's shoulders.

The imprecation psalms articulate a cry from the depths, a cry for justice in the face of human atrocity. Psalm 137 is not so much a call to infanticide as a call for God's judgment to restore a defeated and demoralized people, a judgment that necessarily involves the collapse of hegemonic rule.[13] Hermeneutically, the anguished cry of Psalm 137 gives voice to the suffering of many colonized peoples throughout history. Being uprooted and forced into servitude is not an experience alien to our contemporary, "civilized" world. The psalmist of antiquity speaks out of a condition of pain and powerlessness and thus on behalf of today's refugee, political prisoner, and victim of marital abuse (see Ps 55). The pray-er has no other means except to beseech God in the fervent hope that the imbalance of power will be rectified. For many readers, particularly those who have not experienced injustice, these psalms do not invite prayerful appropriation. Rather, they demand a hearing by giving voice to the oppressed *other*, the one who calls the reader to account.

POSTSCRIPT

THE PSALTER AS TEMPLE

Now that we have explored the Psalms in various ways (mere scratches on the surface, to be sure), it is time to step back and take an all-encompassing look at the Psalter itself. What does it look like? Early on, we discussed the topic of metaphor in the context of biblical poetry, so perhaps it is only appropriate to conclude with an image to "try on" for its coverage of the Psalter as a whole. What metaphor would be most fitting? Is it even possible to imagine one that could adequately cover the Psalter in all its breadth and variety? Any metaphor, like any narrative schema,[1] will highlight only certain aspects of the Psalter while suppressing others, as has always been the case in the history of interpretation.

In his famous letter to Marcellinus, the early bishop of Alexandria, Athanasius (ca. 296–373), likened the Psalter to a mirror:

> Among all the books, the Psalter has certainly a very special grace, a choiceness of quality well worthy to be pondered.... It is like a picture, in which you see yourself portrayed and, seeing, may

understand and consequently form yourself upon the pattern given.... Just as in a mirror, the movements of our own souls are reflected in [the Psalms] and the words are indeed our very own, given us to serve both as a reminder of our changes of condition and as a pattern and model for the amendment of our lives.[2]

With this metaphor, Athanasius captured well the resonance and prescriptive force of the Psalter for readers, both ancient and modern. Even as they offer models of prayer and praise to God, the Psalms reflect some of our deepest concerns, desires, and fears.

Building on this metaphor, John Calvin (1509–1564) called the Psalms "an anatomy of all parts of the soul" because

> there is not an emotion of which anyone can be conscious that is not here represented as in a mirror.... The other parts of Scripture contain the commandments which God enjoined his servant to announce to us. But here [in the Psalms] the prophets...call, or rather draw, each of us to the examination of himself in particular, in order that none of the many infirmities to which we are subject, and of the many vices with which we abound, may remain concealed. It is certainly a rare and singular advantage, when all lurking places are discovered, and the heart is brought into the light, purged from the most baneful infection, hypocrisy.[3]

Taking his cue from Athanasius, Calvin looked into the mirror and found his own soul laid bare. The mirror, he observed, is illuminated, and the image it casts is a deep and discerning look into the inner workings of the conflicted self.

With their related metaphors, both the early church father and the Protestant reformer stress the individual, introspective dimensions of the Psalms. But, of course, there is much more to the Psalter than its mirroring of the human self. The Psalms bear a distinctly corporate dimension. Saint Jerome (c. 347–420), the translator of the Vulgate, offered, shall we say, a more monumental metaphor.

> The Psalter is like a stately mansion [*magna domus*] that has only one key to the main entrance. Within the mansion, however, each separate chamber has its own key. Even though the great key to the grand entrance is the Holy Spirit, still each room without exception has its own smaller key.... The main entrance to the mansion of the Psalter is the first psalm.[4]

158

Jerome's mansion of many rooms appropriately acknowledges the Psalter's great diversity. But I find the image a bit too generic. There is, to quote Athanasius, a "choiceness of quality" about the Psalms that suggests a particular kind of edifice—perhaps a temple, one constructed not from stone but from words.[5] Its entrance is flanked by two pillars: Psalms 1 and 2 (cf. 1 Kgs 7:21-22). Once inside, the listener is caught up in the myriad voices of people addressing God and one another. They are a motley group: kings and prophets, the poor and needy, pilgrims and priests. They are both anonymous and renowned, named and unnamed. All have voice in the Psalms. But regardless of their identities and pedigrees, the voices that populate the Psalter constitute a refuge not of solitude and silence but of impassioned worship and discursive reflection, individually and corporately. The reader joins this earthly cloud of witnesses as they raise their voices to God in petition and praise and to one another in proclamation and instruction. The Psalter is a house of prayer and instruction.

This verbal temple has its own architecture, or structured movement. Earthly kingship yields to divine kingship; the king paves the way to Zion, God's holy abode. And like a worship service, complaint and petition, confession and proclamation, move toward all-encompassing praise: "Let everything that has breath praise YHWH" (150:6). The God of the Psalms is "enthroned on Israel's praises" (22:3). If Psalms 1 and 2 form the entrance to this *templum spirituale,* then Psalms 146–150 represent the capstone of the structure and the culmination of worship. As one proceeds from the entrance to the temple's inner sanctum, the reader of Psalms moves from the conflicts and traumas of the world to the place where God reigns supreme, eliciting universal praise, where all is right with the world. There, at the climax of worship, God is approached, and a whole new world opens up where wickedness is no more and all creation bursts forth with singing. No wonder the rabbis called the Psalter *sēper tĕhillîm,* "The Book of Praises."

As for the Psalter's "temple" foundation,[6] Psalm 1 claims *tôrâ,* God's teaching, as the base upon which the Psalms are built. But, as many of the subsequent psalms make clear, this foundation consists not just of God's word of instruction but also of God's work of salvation and judgment. Together, God's word and work constitute the object of the psalmist's active, creative, discursive "meditation" (1:2). The Psalms, then, are the impassioned, edifying response to God's way in Israel's life and in the life of the world. Whereas other books of the Bible contain God's words and the narratives of God's work, both in history and in creation, the Psalter conveys something of Israel's vociferous response to God—the community's cries and acclamations, its proclamations and discursive reflections. The Psalms present, in short, a sanctuary of shouting and singing.

NOTES

1. Psalms as Poetry: Prosody

1. Jay Parini, *Why Poetry Matters* (New Haven: Yale University Press, 2008), xiv.

2. Quoted in Ellen Davis, "The Soil That Is Scripture," in *Engaging Biblical Authority: Perspectives on the Bible as Scripture* (ed. William P. Brown; Louisville: Westminster John Knox, 2007), 40–41.

3. Quoted in X. J. Kennedy and Dana Gioia, *Literature: An Introduction to Fiction, Poetry, and Drama* (7th ed.; New York: Longman, 1999), 647.

4. Mary Kinzie, *A Poet's Guide to Poetry* (Chicago: University of Chicago Press, 1999), 140.

5. J. P. Fokkelman, *Reading Biblical Poetry: An Introductory Guide* (Louisville: Westminster John Knox, 2001), 15.

6. Ibid.

7. Laurence Perrine, *Sound and Sense: An Introduction to Poetry* (2d ed.; New York: Harcourt, Brace & World, 1963), 3–4.

8. Ibid., 10–11.

9. Kinzie, *A Poet's Guide to Poetry,* 142.

10. See ibid., 787–853.

11. See the superscriptions in Pss 22, 45, 56, 60, 69, and 80.

12. S. E. Gillingham, *The Poems and Psalms of the Hebrew Bible* (Oxford Bible Series; Oxford: Oxford University Press, 1994), 5.

13. Kennedy and Gioia, *Literature,* 651.

14. Kinzie, *A Poet's Guide to Poetry,* 14.

15. Ibid.

16. Ibid., 2.

17. Ibid.

18. Ibid., 14.

19. Kennedy and Gioia, *Literature,* 1011.

20. Kinzie, *A Poet's Guide to Poetry,* 14.

21. See Gillingham, *Poems and Psalms,* 58–59.

161

22. See Fokkelman, *Reading Biblical Poetry*, 18, 24.

23. Wilfred G. E. Watson, *Classical Hebrew Poetry: A Guide to Its Techniques* (JSOTSup 26; Sheffield: JSOT Press, 1986), 92.

24. See Peter W. Flint, *The Dead Sea Psalms Scrolls and the Book of Psalms* (STDJ 17; Leiden: Brill, 1997), 33–34.

25. Robert Lowth, *Lectures on the Sacred Poetry of the Hebrews* (2 vols.; New York: Garland Publishing, 1971 [1787]), 69.

26. Ibid., 68.

27. Ibid., 68–69.

28. Robert Lowth, *Isaiah: A New Translation with a Preliminary Dissertation and Notes, Critical, Philological, and Explanatory* (10th ed.; Boston: William Hilliard; Cambridge: James Munroe and Company, 1834), ix.

29. The quote is "answering one to another in the corresponding lines" (ibid.).

30. Ibid.

31. Ibid.

32. Ibid., xv.

33. The Hebrew word order begins with the independent personal pronoun ("you") followed by the object followed by the verb.

34. Read *nagbîr* for MT *nazkîr*.

35. For a full discussion with examples, see Watson, *Classical Hebrew Poetry*, 333.

36. Kinzie, *A Poet's Guide to Poetry*, 407.

37. James L. Kugel, *The Idea of Biblical Poetry: Parallelism and Its History* (New Haven: Yale University Press, 1981), 8.

38. Adele Berlin, *The Dynamics of Biblical Parallelism* (2d ed.; Grand Rapids: Eerdmans, 2008), 5 (emphasis added).

39. Ibid., 26. For a technical study of grammatical parallelism in Hebrew poetry, see Stephen A. Geller, *Parallelism in Early Biblical Poetry* (Harvard Semitic Monographs 20; Missoula, Mont.: Scholars Press, 1979).

40. Cited in Kennedy and Gioia, *Literature*, 1011.

41. Viktor Shklovsky, "Art as Technique," in *Russian Formalist Criticism* (ed. and trans. Lee T. Lemon and Marion J. Reis; Lincoln: University of Nebraska Press, 1965), 21, quoted in Robert Alter, *The Art of Biblical Poetry*, 10 (emphasis added).

42. Berlin, *The Dynamics of Biblical Parallelism*, 2.

43. Kinzie, *A Poet's Guide to Poetry*, 49.

44. See Gillingham's discussion in *Poems and Psalms*, 3–4.

45. The antecedent is not God (cf. Song 1:16; Ps 81:3; 2 Sam 23:1).

46. Likely referring to "below" the earth, the netherworld.

47. YH is short for YHWH.

48. The choice of the verb *ršh* is phonetically related to *rws̱*, "to run" (see v. 15).

49. Literally, "of the man."

50. Or "wait for his [acts of] fidelity."

51. With the insertion of an additional *mem*, the sentence might have originally read: "Before his cold water stands up," that is, freezes.

52. Read *Ketib*; *Qere* reflects the smoother reading in parallel with *huqqāyw*.

53. In fact, the case has been made that Ps 147 was originally three separate psalms (vv. 1-6, 7-11, 12-20).

54. Note the opening *allelouia* in the Septuagint.

55. See the references to "daughter Zion" and "daughter Jerusalem" in, e.g., Ps 9:14; Isa 1:8; 10:32; 37:22; Jer 6:23; Lam 1:6; 2:13, 15; Mic 4:8; Zech 9:9.

56. For comparable maternal imagery, see Isa 66:6-13.

57. Cf. Gen 18:12; 25:22; 1 Sam 25:37; Jer 23:9; Job 20:14.

58. Not unlike the ancient tradition of the divine word reflected in a Sumero-Akkadian hymn to the moon god Sin, translated by Ferris J. Stevens in *ANET* 385–86 (especially the latter half of the hymn).

2. Psalms as Poetry: Metaphor

1. See the foundational work of Othmar Keel, *The Symbolism of the Biblical World: Ancient Near Eastern Iconography and the Book of Psalms* (trans. Timothy J. Hallet; Winona Lake, Ind.: Eisenbrauns, 1997 [1978]). For discussion of the rhetorical dynamics between ancient iconography and biblical poetry, see William P. Brown, *Seeing the Psalms: A Theology of Metaphor* (Louisville: Westminster John Knox, 2002).

2. Adele Berlin, *The Dynamics of Biblical Parallelism* (2d ed.; Grand Rapids: Eerdmans, 2008), xii; Adele Berlin, "On Reading Biblical Poetry: The Role of Metaphor," in *Congress Volume: Cambridge 1995* (ed. J. A. Emerton; Leiden: Brill, 1997), 25–36. See also P. van Hecke, "Metaphor in the Hebrew Bible. An Introduction," in *Metaphor in the Hebrew Bible* (ed. P. van Hecke; Leuven: University Press, 2005), 1–18; Brown, *Seeing the Psalms*, 4–8.

3. Luis Alonso Schökel, *A Manual of Hebrew Poetics* (trans. Adrian Graffy; Subsidia Biblica 11; Rome: Editrice Pontificio Istituto Biblico, 1988), 95.

4. For a full discussion, see Brown, *Seeing the Psalms*, 3–13.

5. Ellen F. Davis, "Exploding the Limits: Form and Function in Psalm 22," JSOT 53 (1992): 93.

6. The quotation is adapted from Rhys Roberts's translation in Aristotle, *Rhetoric and Poetics* (trans. Rhys Roberts and Ingram Bywater; The Modern Library; New York: Random House, 1954), 185. Cf. *Poetics* 1457b6.

7. Janet Martin Soskice, *Metaphor and Religious Language* (Oxford: Clarendon Press; New York: Oxford University Press, 1985), 15.

8. I. A. Richards, *The Philosophy of Rhetoric* (The Mary Flexner Lectures on the Humanities 3; New York: Oxford University Press, 1965), 96–97.

9. Ibid.

10. Max Black, "More about Metaphor," in *Metaphor and Thought* (ed. Andrew Ortony; Cambridge: Cambridge University Press, 1979), 28.

11. Paul Avis, *God and the Creative Imagination: Metaphor, Symbol and Myth in Religion and Theology* (London / New York: Routledge, 1999), 94.

12. George Lakoff and Mark Turner, *More than Cool Reason: A Field Guide to Poetic Metaphor* (Chicago / London: University of Chicago Press, 1989), 38–39.

13. Lakoff and Turner's theory of metaphor counters the traditional "interaction theory" of I. A. Richards and Max Black, who considered metaphorical movement to be "bidirectional," that is, from target to source *and* from source to target. The above metaphor, for example, makes no claim about the *temporal* dimensions of robbery. Likewise, the universal metaphor "life is a journey" does not construe journeys *as lives* (Lakoff and Turner, *More than Cool Reason*, 131–32). The mapping is only one way.

14. Soskice adopts a modified "interactive" theory of metaphor, specifically an "interanimation" theory (*Metaphor and Religions Language*, 43–51).

15. Lakoff and Turner, *More than Cool Reason*, 50.

16. Ibid., 50–51.

17. For example, "the leg of a chair" and the "flow of electricity." See Soskice, *Metaphor and Religious Language*, 71–83.

18. Ibid., 73.

19. See Earl R. MacCormac, *A Cognitive Theory of Metaphor* (Cambridge / London: Massachusetts Institute of Technology, 1985), 5, 10, who distinguishes metaphor from analogy by the degree to which metaphor conveys a sense of "strangeness."

20. Soskice, *Metaphor and Religious Language*, 26.

21. Ibid., 57–58.

22. See ch. 2 n. 41. This is developed more fully in Robert Alter, *The Art of Biblical Poetry* (New York: Basic Books, 1985), 3–84.

23. Carol A. Newsom, *The Book of Job: A Contest of Moral Imaginations* (Oxford: Oxford University Press, 2003), 236.

24. The term *ṣedeq* serves double duty to designate both protection and righteousness.

25. The translation for *'ak* is debatable (NRSV has "surely"). For the restrictive sense ("only"), see, e.g., 1 Sam 18:8; Isa 45:14; Pss 37:8; 62:6.

26. The verbal form in Hebrew (√ *rdp*) exhibits an ironic intensity that most English translations, including the NRSV, fail to acknowledge (see below).

27. Repoint as *šibtî* (so LXX). MT has "I shall return." For a discussion of the verbal form ("precative perfect"), see Michael L. Barré, "An Unrecognized Precative Construction in Phoenician and Hebrew," *Biblica* 64 (1983): 416. Cf. Pss 27:4*b*; 61:8.

28. LH iv 32; xlviii 95; iv 45. For translation, see Martha T. Roth, *Law Collections from Mesopotamia and Asia Minor* (SBLWAW 6; Atlanta: Scholars Press, 1995), 80, 135.

29. LH xlvii 35-58. Translation based, with slight modifications, on Roth, *Law Collections*, 133.

30. See, e.g., 2 Sam 5:2; 1 Kgs 22:17; 1 Chron 11:12; Ps 100:3.

31. Read *bĕtōm* for MT *kĕtōm* ("like integrity").

32. Read *le'ammô* for MT *lāmô* ("for them").

33. So *Ketib*, the more provocative reading. For syntactical parallels in which the negative particle and the personal pronoun stand elliptically alone, see Job 15:6; 34:33; Gen 45:8; 1 Kgs 18:18; Isa 45:12. The *Qere* reading ("to him") simply summarizes what follows in the verse (see also Pss 79:13; 95:7). It is thus more likely that a copyist changed this elliptical clause to a more familiar formula rather than the reverse. The *Ketib* highlights the aspect of God as creator and that human beings are not autonomous beings, contrary to what the "wicked" or "fools" think, according to other psalms (e.g., 10:4; 14:1).

34. For a more detailed rhetorical analysis of this portion of Ps 42, see William P. Brown, "'Night to Night,' 'Deep to Deep': The Discourse of Creation in the Psalms," in *"My Words Are Lovely": Studies in the Rhetoric of the Psalms* (ed. Robert L. Foster and David M. Howard Jr.; LHB/OTS 467; New York: T & T Clark, 2008), 63–74.

35. Read *'ayyelet* for MT *'ayyāl*, because of haplography and the gender of the following verb. See Ps 22:1; Jer 14:5.

36. Read the attested *wĕ'er'eh* (qal) for MT *wĕ'ērā'eh* (niphal), the latter being a theological correction.

37. See the parallel in v. 11*b*, which bears a plural suffix. Here, the suffixless infinitive construct indicates an indefinite subject.

38. The text appears corrupt; literally, "I passed over/through the throng (*sāk* ?, a hapax legomenon); I walk [hithpael of *ddh*?] (with) them...." The simplest reconstruction is to read *bĕsōk 'addir* + enclitic mem, designating emphatic force. Or the final word may be a plural form reflecting its parallel *'ĕlōhîm*. For *sōk* as YHWH's abode or refuge, see Pss 27:5; 76:4.

39. Another possible translation is: "...and why so stirred up against me?"

40. Read *yĕšû'ōt pānay*. See v. 12; 43:5. MT divides the verse incorrectly.

41. As a rule, this compound particle establishes a tighter, more natural connection between the previous material and what follows than the more generic *lākēn*, both of which are usually translated "therefore." See

also H. Lenhard, "Über den Unterschied zwischen *lkn* und *'l-kn*," *ZAW* 95 (1983): 269–72, who argues that the compound conjunction indicates already progressing consequences, whereas *lākēn* refers only to future activity. In this context, the speaker's current depression *necessarily* recalls an experience of divine presence.

42. Geographically unknown but evidently within the Hermon mountain range.

43. Read *tĕhillâ* for *tĕpillâ* ("prayer"), as evinced in several Hebrew manuscripts.

44. For the iconographical background of this image, see Brown, *Seeing the Psalms*, 149–50.

45. Cf. the verbal root attested in 5:22; 31:35; Isa 51:15.

46. Richard J. Clifford, *Psalms 1–72* (AOTC; Nashville: Abingdon Press, 2002), 216. See also Samuel Terrien, *The Psalms: Strophic Structure and Theological Commentary* (ECC; Grand Rapids: Eerdmans, 2003), 353–54; Erhard S. Gerstenberger, *Psalms Part 1 with an Introduction to Cultic Poetry* (FOTL 14; Grand Rapids: Eerdmans, 1988), 180; Frank-Lothar Hossfeld and Erich Zenger, *Die Psalmen, Psalm 1-50, Kommentar zum Alten Testament mit der Einheitsübersetzung* (Neue Echter Bibel; Würzburg: Echter Verlag, 1993), 269–70; Hans-Joachim Kraus, *Psalms 1-59: A Commentary* (Minneapolis: Augsburg Fortress, 1988), 440; Luis Alonso Schökel, "The Poetic Structure of Psalm 42-43," JSOT 1 (1976): 6–7.

47. Terrien, *Psalms*, 354.

48. Klaus Seybold, *Die Psalmen* (HAT I/15; Tübingen: J.C.B. Mohr [Paul Siebeck], 1996), 176.

49. See Rolf A. Jacobson, *"Many are Saying": The Function of Direct Discourse in the Hebrew Psalter* (JSOTSup 397; London / New York: T & T Clark, 2004), 45.

3. Psalms as Species

1. See the discussion below on Pss 14, 53, 57, 60, and 108.

2. Hermann Gunkel, completed by Joachim Begrich, *Introduction to the Psalms: The Genres of the Religious Lyric of Israel* (trans. James D. Nogalski; Macon, Ga.: Mercer University Press, 1998), 22–221. Although Gunkel places the genre "Songs about YHWH's Enthronement" after "Hymns," he considers it a "small genre," "an appendix to the hymns" (p. 66).

3. Or "thanksgiving song of Israel." Gunkel also included "blessings and cursings," "legends," and "the torah." Ibid., 235–50.

4. The word *nesah* ("forever") at the end of v. 2a suggests a syntactical division. To read the colon as one question makes little sense.

5. So MT. Frequently suggested is the emendation (without textual support) of *'ēsôt* to *'assabôt* (so BHS) for better sense and parallelism. In

psalmic poetry, inner deliberation between the "soul" and the "speaker" is a marker of crisis, such as in Pss 42 and 62. Of course, the possibility of wordplay cannot be ruled out.

6. Literally, "and my foes rejoice that I am shaken."

7. Or "for" (*kî*).

8. The poetic force of the perfect aspect of the verb *gml* suggests enduring, "good-as-done" activity that is characteristic of God, as most exemplified in God's *ḥesed* (v. 6*aa*). But the larger syntax suggests that the speaker's praise is contingent upon deliverance.

9. Namely, dwellers of Sheol, the abode of the dead.

10. The place of the dead or underworld.

11. The hapax legomenon from an otherwise unattested Hebrew verb (*pwn*) is best read as *'āpûgāh* (see Ps 77:3; Hab 1:4 ["grown cold" or "stiff"]). The cohortative form stresses deliberate result.

12. MT: "my friends—darkness." The versions struggle to establish greater parallelism, and a variety of proposals have been made. The simplest approach is to repoint the previous word as a singular, without consonantal emendation. (Thanks to Travis Bott for this suggestion.) This final verse recapitulates and intensifies vv. 7-9.

13. MT reads: "from my deliverance." However, the slight emendation from *mîšû'ātî* to *miššaw'ātî* establishes a stronger parallel with the following phrase.

14. MT vocalizes as an imperative to read, literally, "Roll onto YHWH," perhaps in parallel to Prov 16:3. Consistency with the following verbal suffixes (3ms) suggests an indicative rendering of the verb. However, an abrupt change in person is not unprecedented in poetic texts. See W. Gesenius and E. Kautzsch, *Gesenius' Hebrew Grammar* (trans. A. E. Cowley; 2d ed.; Oxford: Clarendon, 1910), 462.

15. Often proposed is a metathesis of the first two consonants, rendering "mouth" (*ḥikkî* instead of *kōhî*), which would make for better parallelism, but admittedly without textual support.

16. This is the text-critical crux of the psalm, and the number of proposed reconstructions is legion. The translation above simply reflects the MT as it stands, which appears to be elliptical. Reading *kārû* instead of MT *kā'ārî*, the LXX has, "They pierced my hands and my feet." See also the Psalms scroll from Naḥal Hever (XHev/Se 4, frg. 11, line 4), which apparently reads *k'rw* (Peter W. Flint, *The Dead Sea Psalms Scrolls and the Book of Psalms* STDJ 17 [Leiden: Brill, 1997], 43, 83, 88), although this is debatable (see Brent A. Strawn, "Psalm 22:17b: More Guessing," in *JBL* 119 [2000]: 447–48 n. 41). If a verb did indeed drop out through scribal parablepsis, it is impossible to reconstruct. Alternatively, MT's "like a lion" may itself be a scribal mistake of an original verb.

17. Instrumental use of the preposition *min*. See Gen 9:11; Job 7:14; Lev 21:7.

18. For similar usage of this verb, see Hos 2:23; 14:9; Zech 10:6; 118:21. Although the transition from the first to the second colon is quite abrupt, the form of the second verb (qal perfect) indicates a dramatic distinction from the hiphil imperative that opens v. 22. Another possibility that smoothes out the transition is to take the connecting *waw* as explicative: "Save me from the mouth of the lion, for from (or with) the horns of the wild oxen you have responded to me." For the imagery of horns in a ritual context, see 1 Kgs 22:11.

19. So LXX (see following verse); MT features third-person suffixes, in line with the end of v. 25*a* ("afflicted one").

20. The form *yĕhî* suggests that the whole verse should be read in the jussive mood.

21. Verse 29 is textually difficult. The translation is reconstructed.

22. See Ellen F. Davis, "Exploding the Limits: Form and Function in Psalm 22," *JSOT* 53 (1992): 93–105.

23. First suggested by Friedrich Küchler in 1918 and championed by Joachim Begrich in "Das priesterliche Heilsorakel," *ZAW* 52 (1934): 81–92, who drew from the prophetic oracles of Deutero-Isaiah (chs. 40–55) for examples. (Thanks to Brent Strawn for the reference to Küchler.)

24. See the argument made by H. G. M. Williamson in "Reading the Lament Psalms Backwards," in *A God So Near: Essays on Old Testament Theology in Honor of Patrick D. Miller* (ed. Brent A. Strawn and Nancy R. Bowen; Winona Lake, Ind.: Eisenbrauns, 2003), 3–16.

25. For recent explorations, see Ee Kon Kim, *The Rapid Change of Mood in the Lament Psalms* (Seoul: Korea Theological Study Institute, 1985); Brad D. Strawn and Brent A. Strawn, "From Petition to Praise: An Intrapsychic Phenomenon?" (paper presented at the Society of Biblical Literature Annual Meeting, Denver, Col., November 2001); Sung-Hun Lee, "Lament and the Joy of Salvation in the Lament Psalms," in *The Book of Psalms: Composition and Reception* (ed. Peter W. Flint and Patrick D. Miller Jr.; Leiden: Brill, 2005), 224–47; LeAnn Snow Flesher, "Rapid Change of Mood: Oracles of Salvation, Certainty of a Hearing, or Rhetorical Play?" in *"My Words Are Lovely": Studies in the Rhetoric of the Psalms* (ed. Robert L. Foster and David M. Howard Jr.; LHB/OTS 467; New York: T & T Clark, 2008), 33–45.

26. The movement from praise to petition, more typical of psalms outside the biblical literature, casts praise as a motive for divine intervention (see, e.g., the "Great Prayer to Ishtar," in *BM* 2:503–9. See also *ANET* 386–87).

27. Claus Westermann, *Praise and Lament in the Psalms* (trans. Keith R. Crim and Richard N. Soulen; Atlanta: John Knox Press, 1981), 25–35.

28. For whatever reason, the biblical Psalter contains many more individual psalms of thanksgiving than communal ones, perhaps because the

communal ones cross the fine line into corporate psalms of praise. See 65, 67, 75.

29. Literally, "my liver" (*kĕbēdî*). See also Pss 7:6; 16:9; 108:2. MT has "glory," which makes little sense.

4. Psalms as Performance

1. Robert Alter, *The Art of Biblical Poetry* (New York: Basic Books, 1985), 9.

2. Gary A. Anderson, *A Time to Mourn, A Time to Dance: The Expression of Grief and Joy in Israelite Religion* (University Park: Pennsylvania State University Press, 1991).

3. The phrase is borrowed from Yehezkel Kaufmann, *The History of Israelite Religion* (4 vols.; Tel Aviv: Dvir, 1937–1956; Hebrew), 2:476–77. See also Israel Knohl, *The Sanctuary of Silence: The Priestly Torah and the Holiness School* (Minneapolis: Fortress, 1995), 124–64.

4. See 37:7; 46:10; 62:1, 5; 65:1; cf. 39:2, 9; 131:1-3.

5. So MT (literally, "butter / cream"), likely in the sense of vitality or vigor. Other suggestions include "my tongue" (so *HALOT* 253) but without textual support.

6. That is, evaporated or squeezed out (by the weight of God's hand). The verb *hpk* in the niphal can mean everything from "be overthrown" to "be altered or changed."

7. Hebrew *tōp*, "hand drum," typically, but not exclusively, played by women. See Exod 15:20 and Joachim Braun, *Music in Ancient Israel/Palestine: Archaeological, Written, and Comparative Sources* (trans. Douglas W. Stott; Grand Rapids: Eerdmans, 2002), 29–30. For Iron Age terra-cotta representations of female hand drummers, see pp. 120–24.

8. For the powerful effect of this instrument, a ram's horn, see Exod 19:13; Josh 6:4-9.

9. Hebrew *'ûgāb*, most likely a flute instrument. See Braun, *Music in Ancient Israel/Palestine*, 31–32.

10. Hebrew *zēker*, which can also designate the invoked name in worship (Exod 3:15; Isa 26:8; Hos 12:6; Pss 6:6; 97:12; 102:13; 135:13; 146:7).

11. In these instances, *kābôdî* ("my glory") likely reflects an original *kĕbēdî* (30:12; 7:6; 16:9; 108:2).

12. For nature's praise in the Psalms, see Terence E. Fretheim, *God and World in the Old Testament: A Relational Theology of Creation* (Nashville: Abingdon Press, 2005), 249–68; Terence E. Fretheim, "Nature's Praise of God in the Psalms," *Ex Auditu* 3 (1987): 16–30.

13. MT is unclear ("You have magnified, above all your name, your word"). Slight repointing is required: *'al kōl* ("above everything"), so that the pronoun is not in construct with *šimkā* ("your name").

14. Meaning uncertain. Akkadian and Ugaritic cognates bear a discursive meaning ("shout, speak").

15. Read with LXX *nô'ām* for MT *mĕ'ôn* ("habitation"). Cf. Ps 27:4*b*.

16. According to Masoretic punctuation, this clause belongs to the first colon. However, Targum, along with parallelism and syntax, suggests otherwise. The clause serves as protasis for the following.

17. MT reads, "Sacrifices of God are a broken spirit," but the parallelism (e.g., God cast in the vocative) suggests otherwise. The change requires no consonantal emendation.

18. Technically, "small herbivorous terrestrial animals." Cf. Ps 80:14, where this kind of animal is considered a grapevine eater. See Richard Whitekettle, "Bugs, Bunny, or Boar? Identifying the *Zîz* Animals of Psalms 50 and 80," *CBQ* 67 (2005): 250–64.

19. The exegetical challenge is to identify this "sacrifice" either as the typical communion or shared sacrifice, that is, a "thank offering" (Ps 107:22; Lev 7:12-15; 22:29; Amos 4:5; Jonah 2:9 [?]) or as a hymn of thanksgiving (e.g., Pss 26:7; 42:5; 69:31). The verb *zbḥ* literally means "to slaughter" but may be functioning metaphorically in this psalm, as in the following psalm (51:17). In either case, the claim is made that God does not require food. Right sacrifice is more reflective of the worshiper's posture before God than God's need.

20. Specifically, dwell as God's guest or dependent (verb *gwr*).

21. For further explication of ancient Israel's worship and how the Psalms might have figured therein, see John H. Hayes in *Understanding the Psalms* (Eugene, Ore.: Wipf and Stock, 2003 [1976]). For a helpful treatment of psalms and worship that also highlights the history of research, see Jerome F. D. Creach, "The Psalms and the Cult," in *Interpreting the Psalms: Issues and Approaches* (ed. David G. Firth and Philip S. Johnston; Downers Grove, Ill.: Intervarsity Press; Leicester: Apollos, 2005), 119–37. On a broader theological scale, see Walter Brueggemann, *Worship in Ancient Israel: An Essential Guide* (Nashville: Abingdon Press, 2005), esp. 11–85.

22. See Exod 29:38-46; Num 28:1-28; 1 Kgs 18:36; 2 Kgs 16:15. Later Jewish tradition prescribed certain psalms to be sung during the daily services: Ps 24 (Sunday), Ps 48 (Monday), Ps 82 (Tuesday), Ps 94 (Wednesday), Ps 81 (Thursday), Ps 93 (Friday), and Ps 92 (Saturday; see its superscription).

23. Exod 23:14-17; 34:18-26; Lev 23; Deut 16:1-17.

24. See Creach's discussion of the link between "thanksgiving" and the thank offering in "The Psalms and the Cult," 123.

25. Erhard S. Gerstenberger, *Psalms Part 1* (FOTL 15; Grand Rapids: Eerdmans, 1988), 7–8, 14.

26. Martin Buss, "Meaning of Cult and the Interpretation of the Old Testament," *JBR* 32 (1964): 317–25.

27. Sigmund Mowinckel, *The Psalms in Israel's Worship* (trans. D. R. Ap-Thomas; 2 vols; Grand Rapids: Eerdmans; Dearborn, Mich.: Dove Booksellers, 2004 [1962]), 1:106.

28. Ibid., 1:8.

29. See J. J. M. Roberts's positive assessment in "Mowinckel's Enthronement Festival: A Review," in *The Book of Psalms: Composition and Reception* (ed. Peter W. Flint and Patrick D. Miller; VTSup 99; Leiden: Brill, 2005), 97–115.

30. For example, 33:3; 96:1; 98:1; 144:9; and 149:1.

31. Walter Brueggemann, *The Message of the Psalms: A Theological Commentary* (Minneapolis: Augsburg, 1984).

32. See, e.g., Isa 3:4; 38:14.

33. This is where I take deep issue with the prevailing opinion that drives a sharp wedge between "reading" and "performing." Gerald Wilson's claim about the function of Ps 1 is typical: "While Ps 1 as introduction sets the 'tone' for an approach to the Psalter, it indicates this is a collection to be read rather than performed" (Gerald Henry Wilson, *The Editing of the Hebrew Psalter* [SBLDS 76; Chico, Calif.: Scholars Press, 1985], 207). To be sure, Ps 1 orients the reader toward a noncultic appropriation of the Psalter, but the reader remains no passive agent. The Psalms are performed even in the act of reading.

5. Psalms as Collections and Clusters

1. One can, however, speak of general, relative concentrations of certain genres within the Psalter. See the following chapter for discussion.

2. One notable exception is the small group of psalms that bear the label *miktām*, possibly a generic label in some sense (Pss 16, 56–60).

3. See 1 Chron 9:19, 31; 26:1, 19; 2 Chron 20:19; cf. Num 16; 26:11.

4. See 1 Chron 6:39; 15:17; 16:7; 26:1; 2 Chron 5:12; Neh 12:46.

5. See the careful study of Frank-Lothar Hossfeld and Erich Zenger, "The So-Called Elohistic Psalter: A New Solution for an Old Problem," in *A God So Near: Essays on Old Testament Theology in Honor of Patrick D. Miller* (ed. Brent A. Strawn and Nancy R. Bowen; Winona Lake: Ind.: Eisenbrauns, 2003), 35–51.

6. Gerald Henry Wilson, *The Editing of the Hebrew Psalter* (SBLDS 76; Chico, Calif.: Scholars Press, 1985), 190.

7. Pss 72 and 127, both ascribed to Solomon, are part of the Davidic collection and the Songs of Ascents, respectively.

8. The same can be said of the short sayings or proverbs placed within the various collections that comprise most of the book of Proverbs.

9. For example, Pss 5:7; 23:6; 24:7; 26:8; 36:8; 52:8; 65:4; 66:13; 69:9.

10. The superscription reflects an unusual arrangement, as if an original

"A Psalm of David" were broken apart with the insertion of the middle clause (cf. the superscriptions of the surrounding psalms, e.g., 29 and 31).

11. 1 Sam 16:14-23; 18:10; 2 Sam 1:17-27; 22:1; 23:1-7. See also 11QPs[a], col. 17.

12. Solomon is the alleged author of Proverbs and the Wisdom of Solomon.

13. For example, Pss 3, 7, 18, 34, 51, 52, 54, 57, 59, and 63.

14. For a discussion of the eschatological scope of the Psalter, see David C. Mitchell, *The Message of the Psalter: An Eschatological Programme in the Book of Psalms* (JSOTSup 252; Sheffield: Sheffield Academic Press, 1997).

15. See Pss 93, 95–99.

16. See most recently Frank-Lothar Hossfeld and Erich Zenger, "'Wer darf hinaufziehn zum Berg JHWHs?' Zur Redaktionsgeschichte und Theologie der Psalmengruppe 15-24," in *Biblische Theologie und gesellschaftlicher Wandel* (ed. G. Braulik, OSB, W. Grβ, and S. McEvenue; Freiburg: Herder, 1993), 166–82; and Patrick D. Miller, "Kingship, Torah Obedience, and Prayer. The Theology of Psalms 15-24," in *Neue Wege der Psalmenforschung. Für Walter Beyerlin* (ed. K. Seybold and E. Zenger; HBS 1; Freiburg: Herder, 1993), 127–42; William P. Brown, "Here Comes the Sun: The Metaphorical Theology of Psalms 15-24," in *The Composition of the Book of Psalms* (ed. Erich Zenger; BETL 238; Leuven: Peeters Press, 2010), 259–77, from which the following discussion is drawn.

17. In v. 7, the "heart" (literally, "kidneys") designates a special, personal medium through which God instructs the speaker at night.

18. The term is grammatically substantive (see, e.g., Pss 86:14; 119:21, 51, 69, 78, 85, 122; Prov 21:24) and can refer either to the speaker's enemies or to his or her own thoughts and/or actions (see below).

19. Miller, "Kingship, Torah Obedience, and Prayer," 128.

20. Psalm 19, I have discovered, is a favorite text used by pilgrims who reach the summit of the traditional site of Mount Sinai (*Jebel Musa*), near Saint Catherine's Monastery, in time to witness the dawn. How appropriate!

6. Psalms as Corpus

1. See the translation in William G. Braude, *The Midrash on Psalms*, vol. 1 (New Haven: Yale University Press, 1959), 5.

2. 11QPs[a] col. 17, line 11.

3. See Walter Brueggemann, "Bounded by Obedience and Praise: The Psalms as Canon," *JSOT* 50 (1991): 63–92; reprinted in *The Psalms and the Life of Faith* (ed. Patrick D. Miller; Minneapolis: Fortress, 1995), 189–213.

4. Gerald Henry Wilson, *The Editing of the Hebrew Psalter* (SBLDS 76; Chico, Calif.: Scholars Press, 1985), 207.

5. The final book of the Psalter actually marks a minor resurgence of the Davidic psalms, compared to only one psalm in Book III attributed to David (Ps 86) and two in Book IV (Pss 101, 103). Nevertheless, the contrast remains with Book I. See Nancy L. deClaissé-Walford, *Introduction to the Psalms: A Song from Ancient Israel* (St. Louis: Chalice, 2004), 116.

6. Such thematic and editorial distinctions find a measure of convergence with the editorial history of the Psalter. In light of evidence gained from Qumran, it appears that Books I–III of the Hebrew Psalter were actually stabilized before Books IV and V, whose order differs markedly from the one reflected in the Masoretic tradition. See Peter W. Flint, *The Dead Sea Psalms Scrolls and the Book of Psalms* (STDJ 17; Leiden: Brill, 1997), esp. 135–49.

7. Wilson, *Editing of the Hebrew Psalter*, 215.

8. Ibid., 220.

9. Ibid., 227.

10. See deClaissé-Walford, *Introduction*, 129.

11. V. Steven Parrish, *A Story of the Psalms: Conversation, Canon, and Congregation* (Collegeville, Minn.: Liturgical Press, 2003), 16–17. Parrish suggestively pairs Israel's story profiled in the Psalms with the "story of the church," specifically the rise and fall of Christendom.

12. Psalms 110 and 132 of Book V present significant "narrative" bumps in this approach. Both recapture the glory days of the Davidic monarchy and God's covenant. As for Ps 132, Wilson, for example, must argue that the psalm was too well established within the Song of Ascents collection to be "deleted" (*Editing of the Hebrew Psalter*, 225). For an updated argument, see Gerald Henry Wilson, "King, Messiah, and the Reign of God: Revisiting the Royal Psalms and the Shape of the Psalter," in *The Book of Psalms: Composition and Reception* (ed. Peter W. Flint and Patrick D. Miller Jr.; Leiden: Brill, 2005), 396–400. For a critique of this approach, see Norman Whybray, *Reading the Psalms as a Book* (JSOTSup 222; Sheffield: Sheffield Academic Press, 1996).

13. To borrow from Wilson, who argued that while Psalm 1 introduces the Psalter as a whole, Ps 2 was intended to introduce Pss 3–89 (*Editing of the Hebrew Psalter*, 204–8; Wilson, "King, Messiah, and the Reign of God," 394–96). While this may have been the case within the editorial history of the Psalter's development, I would contend that with the Psalter's completion Ps 2 continued to identify themes present throughout the Psalter as we now have it. Indeed, one can argue that Ps 149 resonates well with Ps 2. In any case, current narrative approaches to the Psalms have not given the Psalter's *dual* introduction its due.

14. In the legal sense of "stand up in court" (*HALOT* 1086). The poetic parallel in the verse suggests an arena of judgment. An alternative sense is: "[the wicked] will not rise up in judgment," that is, the wicked will no longer be in a position to render judgment against the righteous.

15. The emphatic rather than causal use of *kî* is preferable, since it signals conclusive corroboration.

16. Wilson, *Editing of the Hebrew Psalter,* 206–7. See, further, Brevard Childs, *Introduction to the Old Testament as Scripture* (Philadelphia: Fortress, 1979), 513; Richard J. Clifford, *Psalms 1–72* (AOTC; Nashville: Abingdon Press, 2002), 40.

17. See the numerous examples in Ps 119, the quintessential *tôrâ* Psalm: vv. 15, 23, 48, 78, 97, and 99. In each case, the object of "meditation" is on YHWH's instructions (e.g., precepts, statutes, decrees, *tôrâ*). Verse 27 even lifts up YHWH's "wondrous works" as an object of "meditation."

18. It is possible that Pss 1 and 119 once formed an editorial *inclusio* in the Psalter's development. See the discussion of the placement of these psalms, along with Ps 19, in James Luther Mays, "The Place of the Torah-Psalms in the Psalter," *JBL* 106 (1987): 3–12.

19. The discursive verb *hgh* is identical to the verb in Ps 1:2*b* ("meditate"), but with an entirely negative meaning. See also Ps 38:13; Prov 24:2.

20. The word is Aramaic (*bar*).

21. Also found in variant forms in Num 14:18; Neh 9:17; Pss 103:8-10; 145:8; Joel 2:13; Jonah 4:2.

22. For the text-critical discussion of this psalm, see William P. Brown, "A Royal Performance: Critical Notes on Psalm 110:3aγ-b," *JBL* 117 (1998): 93–96.

7. Psalms as Theological Anthropology

1. Quoted in Kathleen Norris, "Why the Psalms Scare Us, Part 1," *Christianity Today* 40, 8 (15 July 1996). Cited April 16, 2010. Online: www.christianitytoday.com/ct/1996/july15/6t818a.html.

2. The expression is found in Martin Luther's 1528 "Preface to the Psalter," in *Luther's Works,* vol. 35 (ed. E. Theodore Bachman; Philadelphia: Muhlenberg, 1960), 254.

3. This chapter is based on William P. Brown, "Psalms," in *Theological Bible Commentary* (ed. Gail R. O'Day and David L. Petersen; Louisville: Westminster John Knox, 2009), 170–90.

4. Jerome F. D. Creach, *Yahweh as Refuge and the Editing of the Hebrew Psalter* (JSOTSup 217; Sheffield: Sheffield Academic Press, 1996). In related fashion, James L. Mays argues that God as king constitutes the theological center of the Psalter (*The Lord Reigns: A Theological Handbook to the Psalms* [Louisville: Westminster John Knox, 1994]).

5. William P. Brown, *Seeing the Psalms: A Theology of Metaphor* (Louisville: Westminster John Knox, 2002), 15–53.

6. Hebrew *'ĕlōhîm* refers here to the divine beings that populate the

divine council. See also Ps 82:1 in which both "God" and the "gods" are called *'ĕlōhîm*. In Job 1–2, they are referred to as "the sons of God" (*bĕnê hā'ĕlōhîm* ; 1:6; 2:1).

7. See 6:5*b*; 88:10-12, but cf. 115:17; 139:8*b*.

8. See James L. Mays, "The Self in the Psalms and the Image of God," in *Teaching and Preaching the Psalms* (ed. Patrick D. Miller and Gene M. Tucker; Louisville: Westminster John Knox, 2006), 56.

9. For further discussion, see Serene Jones, "'Soul Anatomy': Calvin's Commentary on the Psalms," in *Psalms in Community: Jewish and Christian Textual, Liturgical, and Artistic Traditions* (ed. Harold W. Attridge and Margot E. Fassler; Society of Biblical Literature Symposium Series 25; Atlanta: Society of Biblical Literature, 2003), 265–84.

10. See Exod 34:6-7; Pss 86:15; 103:8; 145:8.

11. For a study of happiness in the Psalms, see William P. Brown, "Happiness and Its Discontents in the Psalms," in *The Bible and the Pursuit of Happiness* (ed. Brent A. Strawn, forthcoming).

12. See Exod 40:34; Num 20:6; Pss 24:7-10; 26:8; 78:60-61; 96:8.

13. Erich Zenger, *A God of Vengeance? Understanding the Psalms of Divine Wrath* (Louisville: Westminster John Knox, 1996), 47–50.

Postscript

1. See chap. 6.

2. Saint Athanasius, "Appendix: The Letter of St. Athanasius to Marcellinus on the Interpretation of the Psalms," in *On the Incarnation* (2d ed.; Crestwood, NY: St. Vladimir's Seminary, 2003), 103, 106. Elsewhere, Athanasius refers to the Psalter as a garden, one that is particularly diverse, unlike those gardens that constitute other books of the Bible.

3. John Calvin, *Commentary on the Book of Psalms* (trans. J. Anderson; 5 vols.; Edinburgh: Calvin Translation Society, 1945; Grand Rapids: Eerdmans, 1949), 1:xxxvi–xxxvii.

4. Jerome, "Homily 1," in *The Homilies of Saint Jerome* (trans. Sister Marie Liguori Ewald, I.H.M.; vol. 48 of The Fathers of the Church; Washington, D.C.: The Catholic University of America Press, 1964), 3.

5. For a detailed examination of this metaphor in light of the Psalter's structure and movement, see the essay by Bernd Janowski, to which I am indebted: "Ein Tempel aus Worten: Zur theologischen Architektur des Psalters" in *The Composition of the Book of Psalms* (ed. Erich Zenger; BETL 238; Leuven: Peeters, 2010), 279–306.

6. Or, in keeping with the "book" metaphor, its spine.

SELECT BIBLIOGRAPHY

Commentaries and Translations

Allen, Leslie C. *Psalms 101–150.* 2d ed. Word Biblical Commentary 21. Nashville: Thomas Nelson, 2002.

Alter, Robert. *The Book of Psalms: A Translation with Commentary.* New York: W. W. Norton, 2007.

Anderson, A. A. *Psalms.* 2 vols. New Century Bible. Grand Rapids: Eerdmans, 1972.

Briggs, Charles Augustus, and Emilie Grace Briggs. *A Critical and Exegetical Commentary on the Book of Psalms.* 2 vols. International Critical Commentary. Edinburgh: T & T Clark, 1906–1907.

Clifford, Richard J. *Psalms 1–72.* Abingdon Old Testament Commentaries. Nashville: Abingdon Press, 2002.

———. *Psalms 73–150.* Abingdon Old Testament Commentaries. Nashville: Abingdon Press, 2003.

Craigie, Peter C. *Psalms 1–50.* Word Biblical Commentary 19. Waco: Word, 1983.

Dahood, Mitchell. *Psalms.* 3 vols. Anchor Bible 16-17A. Garden City, N.Y.: Doubleday, 1966, 1968, 1970.

Eaton, John. *The Psalms: A Historical and Spiritual Commentary with an Introduction and New Translation.* London: T & T Clark, 2003.

Gerstenberger, Erhard S. *Psalms, Part I: With An Introduction to Cultic Poetry.* Forms of Old Testament Literature 14. Grand Rapids: Eerdmans, 1988.

———. *Psalms, Part 2, and Lamentations.* Forms of Old Testament Literature 15. Grand Rapids: Eerdmans, 2001.

Goldingay, John. *Psalms.* 3 vols. Baker Commentary on the Old

Testament Wisdom and Psalms. Grand Rapids: Baker Academic, 2006–2008.

Grogan, Geoffrey W. *Psalms.* The Two Horizons Old Testament Commentary. Grand Rapids: Eerdmans, 2008.

Hossfeld, Frank-Lothar, and Erich Zenger. *Psalms 2: A Commentary on Psalms 51–100.* Edited by Klaus Baltzer. Hermeneia. Minneapolis: Fortress, 2005.

Kraus, Hans-Joachim. *Psalms 1–59: A Continental Commentary.* Minneapolis: Fortress, 1993.

———. *Psalms 60–150: A Continental Commentary.* Minneapolis: Fortress, 1993.

Limburg, James. *Psalms.* Westminster Bible Companion. Louisville: Westminster John Knox, 2000.

Mays, James L. *Psalms.* Interpretation, a Bible Commentary for Teaching and Preaching. Louisville: Westminster John Knox, 1994.

McCann, J. Clinton, Jr. "The Book of Psalms: Introduction, Commentary, and Reflections." Pages 641–1280 in volume 4 of *The New Interpreter's Bible.* Edited by L. E. Keck et al. Nashville: Abingdon Press, 1998.

Schaefer, Konrad, OSB. *Psalms.* Berit Olam. Collegeville, Minn.: Liturgical Press, 2001.

Tate, Marvin E. *Psalms 51–100.* Word Biblical Commentary 20. Dallas: Word, 1990.

Terrien, Samuel L. *The Psalms: Strophic Structure and Theological Commentary.* Eerdmans Critical Commentary. Grand Rapids: Eerdmans, 2003.

Weiser, Artur. *The Psalms: A Commentary.* Old Testament Library. Philadelphia: Westminster, 1962.

Wilson, Gerald H. *Psalms, Volume 1.* NIV Application Commentary. Grand Rapids: Zondervan, 2002.

Monographs and Edited Volumes

Alter, Robert. *The Art of Biblical Poetry.* New York: Basic Books, 1985.

Anderson, Bernhard W., with Steven Bishop. *Out of the Depths: The Psalms Speak for Us Today.* 3d ed. Louisville: Westminster John Knox, 2000.

Attridge, Harold W., and Margot E. Fassler, eds. *Psalms in*

Community: Jewish and Christian Textual, Liturgical, and Artistic Traditions. Society of Biblical Literature Symposium Series 25. Atlanta: Society of Biblical Literature, 2003.

Bellinger, W. H., Jr. *Psalms: Reading and Studying the Book of Praises.* Peabody: Hendrickson, 1990.

Berlin, Adele. *The Dynamics of Biblical Parallelism.* 2d ed. Grand Rapids: Eerdmans, 2008.

Brown, William P. *Seeing the Psalms: A Theology of Metaphor.* Louisville: Westminster John Knox, 2002.

Brueggemann, Walter. *The Message of the Psalms: A Theological Commentary.* Minneapolis: Augsburg, 1984.

————. *Abiding Astonishment: Psalms, Modernity, and the Making of History.* Louisville: Westminster John Knox, 1991.

————. *The Psalms and the Life of Faith.* Edited by Patrick D. Miller. Minneapolis: Fortress, 1995.

————. *Worship in Ancient Israel: An Essential Guide.* Nashville: Abingdon Press, 2005.

deClaissé-Walford, Nancy L. *Reading from the Beginning: The Shaping of the Hebrew Psalter.* Macon, Ga.: Mercer University Press, 1997.

————. *Introduction to the Psalms: A Song from Ancient Israel.* St. Louis: Chalice, 2004.

Creach, Jerome F. D. *Yahweh as Refuge and the Editing of the Hebrew Psalter.* Journal for the Study of the Old Testament: Supplement Series 217. Sheffield: Sheffield Academic Press, 1996.

————. *The Destiny of the Righteous in the Psalms.* St. Louis: Chalice Press, 2008.

Crenshaw, James L. *The Psalms: An Introduction.* Grand Rapids: Eerdmans, 2001.

Firth, David G., and Philip S. Johnston, eds. *Interpreting the Psalms: Issues and Approaches.* Downers Grove, Ill.: Intervarsity Press; Leicester: Apollos, 2005.

Flint, Peter W. *The Dead Sea Psalms Scrolls and the Book of Psalms.* Studies on the Texts of the Desert of Judah 17. Leiden: Brill, 1997.

Flint, Peter W., and Patrick D. Miller, eds. *The Book of Psalms: Composition and Reception.* Supplements to Vetus Testamentum 99. Leiden: Brill, 2005.

Fokkelman, J. P. *Reading Biblical Poetry: An Introductory Guide.* Louisville: Westminster John Knox, 2001.

Foster, Robert L., and David M. Howard, eds. *"My Words Are Lovely": Studies in the Rhetoric of the Psalms.* New York: T & T Clark, 2008.

Gillingham, S. E. *The Poems and Psalms of the Hebrew Bible.* Oxford Bible Series. Oxford: Oxford University Press, 1994.

Gunkel, Hermann. *The Psalms: A Form-Critical Introduction.* Translated by Thomas M. Horner. Philadelphia: Fortress, 1967.

Gunkel, Hermann, completed by Joachim Begrich. *Introduction to Psalms: The Genres of the Religious Lyric of Israel.* Translated by James D. Nogalski. Macon, Ga.: Mercer University Press, 1998.

Hayes, John H. *Understanding the Psalms.* Eugene, Ore.: Wipf and Stock, 2003 (1976).

Holladay, William L. *The Psalms through Three Thousand Years: Prayerbook of a Cloud of Witnesses.* Minneapolis: Fortress, 1993.

Keel, Othmar. *The Symbolism of the Biblical World: Ancient Near Eastern Iconography and the Book of Psalms.* Translated by Timothy J. Hallet. Winona Lake, Ind.: Eisenbrauns, 1997 [1978].

Kinzie, Mary. *A Poet's Guide to Poetry.* Chicago: University of Chicago Press, 1999.

Kraus, Hans-Joachim. *Theology of the Psalms.* Translated by Keith Crim. Minneapolis: Augsburg, 1986.

Kugel, James L. *The Idea of Biblical Poetry: Parallelism and Its History.* New Haven, Conn.: Yale University Press, 1981.

Mays, James L. *The Lord Reigns: A Theological Handbook to the Psalms.* Louisville: Westminster John Knox, 1994.

———. *Teaching and Preaching the Psalms.* Edited by Patrick D. Miller and Gene M. Tucker. Louisville: Westminster John Knox, 2006.

McCann, J. Clinton, Jr. *A Theological Introduction to the Book of Psalms: The Psalms as Torah.* Nashville: Abingdon Press, 1993.

———, ed. *The Shape and Shaping of the Psalter.* Journal for the Study of the Old Testament: Supplement Series 159. Sheffield: Sheffield Academic Press, 1993.

Miller, Patrick D. *Interpreting the Psalms.* Philadelphia: Fortress, 1986.

———. *They Cried to the Lord: The Form and Theology of Biblical Prayer.* Minneapolis: Fortress, 1994.

Mitchell, David C. *The Message of the Psalter: An Eschatological Programme in the Book of Psalms.* Journal for the Study of the

Old Testament: Supplement Series 252. Sheffield: Sheffield Academic Press, 1997.

Mowinckel, Sigmund. *The Psalms in Israel's Worship*. Translated by D. R. Ap-Thomas. Grand Rapids: Eerdmans; Dearborn, Mich.: Dove, 2004 [1962].

Nasuti, Harry P. *Defining the Sacred Songs: Genre, Tradition and the Post-Critical Interpretation of the Psalms*. Journal for the Study of the Old Testament: Supplement Series 218. Sheffield: Sheffield Academic Press, 1999.

Parrish, V. Stephen. *A Story of the Psalms: Conversation, Canon, and Congregation*. Collegeville, Minn.: Liturgical Press, 2003.

Petersen, David L., and Kent Harold Richards. *Interpreting Hebrew Poetry*. Guides to Biblical Scholarship. Minneapolis: Fortress, 1992.

Reid, Stephen Breck. *Listening In: A Multicultural Reading of the Psalms*. Nashville: Abingdon Press, 1997.

Schökel, Luis Alonso. *A Manual of Hebrew Poetics*. Translated by Adrian Graffy. Subsidia Biblica 11. Rome: Editrice Pontificio Istituto Biblico, 1988.

Smith, Mark S. *The Psalms: The Divine Journey*. New York: Paulist, 1987.

Swenson, Kristin M. *Living through Pain: Psalms and the Search for Wholeness*. Waco: Baylor University Press, 2005.

Van Harn, Roger E., and Brent A. Strawn, eds. *Psalms for Preaching and Worship*. Grand Rapids, Mich.: Eerdmans, 2009.

Vos, Cas J. A. *Theopoetry of the Psalms*. London: T & T Clark, 2005.

Watson, Wilfred G. E. *Classical Hebrew Poetry: A Guide to its Techniques*. Journal for the Study of the Old Testament: Supplement Series 26. Sheffield: JSOT Press, 1986.

Westermann, Claus. *The Psalms: Structure, Content, and Message*. Minneapolis: Augsburg, 1980.

———. *Praise and Lament in the Psalms*. Translated by Keith R. Crim and Richard N. Soulen. Atlanta: John Knox, 1981.

Whybray, Norman. *Reading the Psalms as a Book*. Journal for the Study of the Old Testament: Supplement Series 222. Sheffield: Sheffield Academic Press, 1996.

Wilson, Gerald H. *The Editing of the Hebrew Psalter*. Society of Biblical Literature Dissertation Series 76. Chico, Calif.: Scholars Press, 1985.

Zenger, Erich. *A God of Vengeance? Understanding the Psalms of Divine Wrath*. Louisville: Westminster John Knox, 1996.

INDEX